Between GRIT and GRACE

The Art of Being Feminine and Formidable

Lessons from Bossy, Caring, Fearless, Vulnerable,
Relentless, Forgiving Women at the Top

D0051846

Sasha K. Shillcutt, MD

Health Communications, Inc.
Boca Raton, Florida

www.hcibooks.com

**Library of Congress Cataloging-in-Publication Data
is available through the Library of Congress**

© 2020 Sasha K. Shillcutt, MD

ISBN-13: 978-07573-2347-8 (Paperback)
ISBN-10: 07573-2347-2 (Paperback)
ISBN-13: 978-07573-2348-5 (ePub)
ISBN-10: 07573-2348-0 (ePub)

Publisher: Health Communications, Inc.
          1700 NW 2nd Ave.
          Boca Raton, FL 33432–1653

Cover design by Larissa Hise Henoch
Interior design and formatting by Lawna Patterson Oldfield

Praise for

Between GRIT and GRACE

"In this remarkable book, Dr. Sasha Shillcutt eloquently navigates the rocky terrain associated with being a strong, intelligent, and empathic woman. Focusing on grit and grace, she entertains readers with stories that will make them laugh out loud and leaves them with solid advice that they can apply to their own lives. Great leaders do wear lipstick, and in the time-honored tradition of women supporting other women, this book is one that you'll want to pass on to your colleagues, mentees, and friends."

> —**Julie Silver, MD**, associate professor, Harvard Medical School,
> director of a women's leadership course for physicians, and
> author of *You Can Heal Yourself: A Guide to Physical
> and Emotional Recovery After Injury or Illness*

"Dr. Sasha Shillcutt is a whirlwind of down-to-earth, commonsense advice for every woman aspiring to be fierce, fearless, and forward-looking. She has an innate sense of how to combine being a successful physician, wife, mom, blogger, and mentor with an edgy dose of badass empowerment. This book is a prescription to heal what ails all of us!"

> —**Deborah R. Gilg, JD,** retired U.S. Attorney for Nebraska

"Dr. Sasha Shillcutt writes in a style that makes you feel like you are getting great advice from your best friend. She connects in a way that makes you feel like she speaks to your soul. She gets you. She is you. Dr. Shillcutt is a fearless innovative leader and a phenomenal physician, mother, wife, and writer. She balances all these facets with imperfectly beautiful grace. Finding Dr. Shillcutt and joining her tribe truly changed my life in so many ways. I am a better physician mother, wife, and friend because of her brilliance and wisdom."

> —**Brittney Terry, DO**, pediatrician

"Dr. Sasha Shillcutt is uniquely qualified to write on the topic of authentic leadership as a woman. Not only is she a national leader in her field in medicine, but she has also managed to create a group, which has grown to thousands, comprised of women physicians who support, encourage, and uplift each other, from all ends of the country. Her authenticity is palpable, and her willingness to be transparent with both her successes and failures as a woman, wife, mother, physician, and friend has inspired many of us to reach for heights in our personal and professional lives that we may not have otherwise."

—**D'Anna Mullins, MD, PhD,** hematology and oncology

"Dr. Sasha Shillcutt is an extraordinary woman, physician, leader, and entrepreneur. Her words are eloquent, showcasing both her vulnerability and strength. She has a strong passion for elevating women around her, encouraging them to be their best selves. Her book *Between Grit and Grace* will be a must-read for anyone who wants to be inspired to be authentic, be visionary, and be brave."

—**Rakhee K. Bhayani, MD,** associate professor of medicine,
Washington University School of Medicine

"Dr. Shillcutt is a true role model for countless women on how to lead authentically. Dr. Shillcutt is a strong, decisive, and confident leader. She has united women by sharing her own true opportunities and challenges, and this transparency has served as the nidus for so many women to grow in their own careers, personal life, and wellness. Dr. Shillcutt writes from the heart, with such grace, and is wise beyond her years. I have always been inspired when she puts pen to paper, as the resulting product is always inspiring."

—**Amy S. Oxentenko, MD, FACP, FACG, AGAF,** professor of medicine,
Mayo Clinic, gastroenterology and hepatology

"Dr. Sasha Shillcutt has a unique talent for leading women to be their true, authentic selves. As a physician educator, she is strong, well respected, and hardworking. As a wife and mother, she is giving and kindhearted. Despite being a busy physician and mother, she continues to uplift and encourage other women to achieve their individual goals and potential. Using personal narratives, humor, and her intellect, Dr. Shillcutt prescribes straightforward, manageable techniques for every woman to discover their inner moxie!"

—**Shivani Mukkamala, MD,** assistant professor
of anesthesiology, Emory University

TO LANCE—
FOR LIGHTING THE PATH
TOWARD MY AUTHENTIC SELF,
AND LOVING ME THROUGH
ALL THE DETOURS.

AND TO SAMUEL,
ASHER, SOPHIA, AND LEVI—
YOU ARE THE BEST
OF MY LIFE.

I will no longer act as if
I were less than the whole person
I know myself inwardly to be.

—**Rosa Parks**[1]

CONTENTS

Acknowledgments ix

Introduction 1

Chapter 1 Kind and Obedient and Compliant 5

Chapter 2 Your Internal Voice: Frenemy vs. Fangirl 25

Chapter 3 One of the Boys…Not 45

Chapter 4 Everything to Everyone but
           Nothing to Myself 67

Chapter 5 Brave Enough to Be Me 93

Chapter 6 Be Bossy; It's Okay 119

Chapter 7 Finding Your Five 141

Chapter 8 An Imposter Among Us 163

Chapter 9 Leadership and Lipstick 181

Chapter 10 The Safety of the Shore 201

Notes 221

Resources 227

About the Author 229

ACKNOWLEDGMENTS

I have wanted to write a book for as long as I can remember. I love to read, and I spent most of my childhood hiding with a book, lost in a world of inspectors and green gables and women flying planes in WWII. When I was finally brave enough to say the words out loud, *I want to write a book*, they had been living in my head for a long time. I don't think I ever felt as vulnerable as when I claimed those words; it was like handing a newborn baby over to a five-year-old.

Do not drop her; she is fragile.

I was smart enough to hand my dream over to a well-known author, Dr. Julie Silver. I knew she wouldn't drop the baby, and I also knew she wouldn't feed me a line of false pleasantries or empty lies.

She not only held my dream, but she also fed it. She connected me with wonderful resources and told me to *persist*. To Julie, thank you for the honest feedback, the priceless advice, and for helping me and so many others through your Harvard writing course. You are pure magic.

To Martha Murphy, thank you for your superb editorial guidance and for encouraging me to write in my authentic voice. I am a better writer because of you. To Jeanne, thank you for your diligence to see this project come to life and believing a woman from Nebraska had something to say. Your tenacity is so appreciated. To Christine, thank you for your excellent editorial guidance. To Nicole, thank you for being equal parts cheerleader and wordsmith; for assuring me a hundred times that someone would find my words interesting. To Michelle, thank you for your loyalty and fixing all my mistakes with grace.

To my sisters: Dr. Mina Lee, Dr. Ali Novitsky, Aimee Lowe, Laurie Baedke, Dr. Sybile Val, Dr. Shivani Mukkamala, Dr. Brittney Terry, Dr. Jennifer Best, Dr. Casey Lewis, Dr. Julie Smith, Dr. Michelle Otero, Jayme Small, Dr. Tara Brakke, Dr. Stephanie Randall, Dr. J. Schoemaker, Dr. Gail Yanney, Aimee Lowe, and honestly so many others . . . thank you for seeing me for who I strive to be, not for who I am.

To my family, thank you for all the countless times you stepped in . . . Michaela, Pack, Leah, TJ, Amy, Deanna, and Mike . . . thank you for the endless car rides, meals, loving my kids, and the grace upon grace upon grace that is required to do life with Sasha. You are my biggest blessing, and I am only able to pour into others because you pour into me.

To my mom, thank you for teaching me to be kind first and ask questions later. And to my father, thank you for making me challenge the status quo and define my own success. And to Grandma Dee, thank you for teaching me the power of red lipstick and being authentic before it was popular.

To my SMD tribe: thank you for being living proof that strong women can support other strong women and for showing me the best of humankind; and for inspiring me every day to live brave.

To Lance, Samuel, Asher, Sophia, and Levi, thank you for being quiet when you wanted to be loud so I could concentrate, for refilling my coffee cup umpteen times, and for feeding my soul.

And to my Creator, thank you for making me brave.

INTRODUCTION

I walked down the long hotel hallway before entering the conference room, whispering to myself my usual pep talk. "Don't speak too fast. Don't say your first idea out loud...wait until the end. Don't forget to smile. Don't correct any of the power players, even if they say something that is incorrect. Don't get upset when someone takes credit for your idea. Just be glad you are here. You are the only woman they invited, after all."

This scenario plays in my head over and over. Why was I suddenly coaching myself to be smaller than who I was? I was there because I deserved to be. I was there because I had the experience, expertise, and knowledge to add to the conversation. Why was I holding back my ideas, my voice, and my authenticity?

I was experienced. I was educated. And the truth was, I had accomplished more in the span of my career than 90 percent of the men in the room. Why was I being less than who I knew I could be? Why was I shrinking? Why was I hiding?

I wrote this book because over the years I have witnessed countless women withdraw and become less of themselves to please everyone around them. I have watched them hide their greatest attributes, swallow their words, and conceal their ideas and innovation and leadership. I have observed women struggle to please everyone else, and give away piece after piece of themselves, only to end up completely empty.

I have experienced this myself: trying to be more, do more, and learn more. *Be more of a leader*, but not too strong. *Be more collaborative*, but not too inviting. The message to women is clear: be *more*. I wrote this book to challenge the status quo. I wrote it for women to take one big collective breath and say ... *we are enough*.

Women do not need to be *more* of anything—other than ourselves. We are enough.

Why Grit and Grace?

I love being a woman. I always have. Even during the times I've been overlooked when seeking a promotion—simply because I wasn't a man—I've never thought, *Oh, wouldn't it be great to be a guy?* I also love and value men. My best friend is a phenomenal man who happens to be the father of my children, three of the four of whom are boys. One of my most important mentors in medicine is a man.

None of that changes the fact that this book is written for women; it is written for a group of individuals I see often trying to transform their inner She-Ra into something that is accepted in a male-dominated world. It is written for a group of beautiful souls whom I often see overshadowed by the normal, the ordinary, and the status quo. This book is a calling to live authentically, to be who you are at the very core of your being because that is who the world *deserves to know*. It is about prevailing and being brave enough to define your own personal and professional success, no matter how different it is with those around you. It is about owning your gritty side while, at the same time, showing grace.

Women *can* be feminine and formidable. We can lead revolutions one minute and comfort those who follow us the next. We can rule and collaborate, but if we want success, we must get comfortable living in the space *between* grit and grace. Know this: it's okay to be kind *and* badass.

If you are a woman who has ever thought, *Why am I not enough?* This book is for you. If you are a woman who has ever been overlooked, underestimated, undervalued, and overstretched, this book is for you. Each chapter will guide you strategically through a set of internal reflections built on both data and real-life stories from women in the trenches. I've chosen *real* women; women who are both messy and brilliant, whom you will identify with and whose stories will leave you inspired and with a sense of hope. Throughout each chapter, you will be given a series of questions, journal exercises, and quizzes to make you think—challenging you to go inside to the core of who you are. If you are a woman who has ever found herself completely empty, emotionally depleted, and physically burned out, this book is for you. I understand because I have been there. It is why I wrote this book, why I started Brave Enough, and why I am sharing a call to courage with you.

As I found my own path to authenticity, I realized it is crucial to success. I've learned a lot about grit and grace and the space between them. And I realized that my life mission was to share what I've learned both from so many women who have gone before me and from my own life after the times I've fallen down yet gotten back up. Here are the lessons—beautiful, messy truths from bossy, caring, fearless, vulnerable, relentless, forgiving, smart, humble women at the top.

Chapter 1

Kind and Obedient and Compliant

If you just set out to be liked, you would be
prepared to compromise on anything at any time
and you would achieve nothing.

—*Margaret Thatcher*[1]

The Likability Trap

W omen, like men, are complex beings. We have unique characteristics, distinct likes and tastes, and specific goals. We are curious beings, and what motivates us toward a goal one day may steer us in a different direction the next. We were created to be this way, and yet, we are not allowed to be. Women typically learn that success requires the ability to walk a tightrope of what is acceptable. We are often labeled as being moody, emotional, and difficult to understand when we act outside the normal confines of societal cues to stay in the margin of expectation. While we as women are all unique, different in many ways, we are often not allowed to express our authentic selves without backlash. This internal conflict with wanting to be liked, and also wanting to be successful, often leads us to debilitating stress and burnout. When we act authentically, we can suffer harsh consequences and receive feedback that makes us force our authentic selves back into hiding.

It takes immense courage for women to live in the way of their authentic selves. Whether it is working more to achieve the promotion you've always wanted or working less to pursue a life passion, the self-actualization of choosing to define your own success is not easy. It can be extremely difficult and requires a daily dose of bravery. It requires you to be brave enough to take the tiny yet deliberate next step forward. Purposely, cautiously, and yet courageously.

One day, as a junior anesthesiologist looking for guidance, I sat in the office of my former chairman. I was struggling to confront a senior male surgeon about a patient issue. I was thirty-two years old, pregnant with my third child, and working sixty-five hours a week. I was trying to figure out how to balance the life of a full-time cardiac anesthesiologist with the demands of being a full-time parent and wife. I felt as if all eyes were on me, but there was very little support or room to make mistakes. The conflict with a male surgeon who had decades more seniority than me made me feel anxious, small, and powerless.

"Sasha," my mentor said, "there comes a point in every person's career when you have to decide to come out of the dugout. It's how you earn respect." His words stuck with me. Women graduate from college, like men. We earn degrees and complete internships and gain experience, just like our male colleagues. But so very often as women, we never "come out of the dugout," as my chairman described. And when we do, we pay the price.

The last thing I wanted to do after working grueling hours in the operating room taking care of critically ill patients—while trying to keep my own two children safe, fed, and clothed—was have a difficult conversation with a work colleague who peered down at my five-foot three-inch self, often from over the drapes, and let me know his opinion of me. But I had to stand up for my own intellect, and thus for my patients, if I was to gain respect and be the doctor I knew I was. I begrudgingly confronted him one afternoon and could barely hear his response over the sound of my beating heart. The internal conflict was ever so present: I wanted to be liked, but I also wanted to be successful. Why did I feel like I couldn't be both?

After so many years, I had finished all my schooling and on-the-job training and finally found my niche in medicine. I was ready to put to use all the experience I had earned and all the knowledge I had learned. I was determined to be strong, decisive, direct, and caring. As a professional woman, I was supposed to keep my cool, deliver above and beyond what was necessary to prove myself among the men, all while looking perfect and being approachable. You know, I was supposed to be a little bit Wonder Woman, a little bit Margaret Thatcher, and a touch of Reese Witherspoon to soften the edges. On top of it all, I was also supposed to be a terrific mom, feed my family only organic food, and have the wit of Clair Huxtable and the energy of Carol Brady.

Between my work and home responsibilities, I was failing. I was constantly struggling to find that perfect center between two vital yet seemingly opposite traits: *grit* and *grace*. When I found myself acting with grace, I was lacking grit. I'd take control of a work situation with my voice and resolve, only to look around the room and wonder which nurse or technician I'd likely offended with my direct tone. I'd grieve the loss of a patient behind closed doors, with tears streaming down my face, praying no one witnessed my crying and thus labeled me as weak or, even worse, "emotional."

No matter how hard I tried, I found myself in a constant internal battle. I was pulled back and forth by the conflict in my mind, of wanting to exert my influence and ideas yet do so in a matter not to upset my environment. I wanted to be two things: my authentic self, who was a leader, and my collaborative self, who was kind and approachable. *Why couldn't these two parts of me seem to coexist? What was I doing wrong?*

Knowing Oneself: The Key to Strength

This constant internal conflict left me feeling unsatisfied, self-critical, and ultimately burned out. The more I tried to grasp the perfect balance between gritty and graceful, the more pressure I put on myself as I tried to achieve at an increasingly higher level. Maybe if I could just achieve a little more, shine a little brighter, I'd find that magic mix. I'd be accepted and likable and perfect.

To understand our internal battles, we need to understand how we are standing on the battlefield to begin with. We must ask the hard questions, the ones we try not to think about as we drift off to sleep. So, my friend, let's open up those questions. Let's unearth those very thorny and sticky issues. Over the next few chapters, let's ask ourselves *why*.

Why do we women find it hard to stand up for ourselves? Why do we often suffer consequences for being clear and direct in our communication? There are several reasons, and I want you to know when you feel inadequate to stand up for yourself or others, afraid to speak, or experience anxiety when you do, it doesn't mean you are weak, afraid, or not enough. We've all been there; your experiences, your thoughts, and your reactions are *normal*.

One of the most important things we can do as women is to understand ourselves and what drives our behaviors. If we want to achieve our goals, live our passions, and thrive in our workplaces and homes, we must understand *why* we think the way we do.

Understanding why we hold back when we want to take action or why we remain silent when we have a great idea is the key to unearthing our strength. To find our voice, and to understand our makeup and how we relate to others, we must go back to how we experienced success during our formative years as young girls. If we can understand why we often have both internal conflict and external pushback when we exert our leadership, we can change our thoughts. Why should we do this? Because changing our thoughts leads to two things: internal peace and outward confidence.

And isn't that what we most want to do? To feel confident to change our actions, to live the priorities we know are right, to share our ideas, and to lead? To go forward, sometimes we have to go back.

Understanding Our Confidence

In first grade, I attended a school where our classroom was in a portable trailer adjacent to the main building, which was under construction. About fifteen minutes before lunch, our teacher would select two students to collect our lunch milk from the main building. All morning, I would sit in my seat and try not to fidget. I would raise my hand, do my best to speak only when called on, and fight off the giggles—all for the slightest chance to be chosen for milk duty. Bringing that crate back to my classmates felt like I'd won the lottery. Instilled in me from a young age by both my parents and teachers was the idea that if I wanted to succeed, I needed to be obedient. I had to be quiet, raise my hand, and not cause a ruckus. Being selected would mean I was the best, and, in my mind, that could happen only if I followed the unwritten rules.

My experiences are not unique. As young girls, we were rewarded for obedience, following the rules, quietly raising our hands, and being compliant. We earned gold stars and blue ribbons for these behaviors. We were rewarded for actions that forged connections and encouraged collaboration but not necessarily for exhibiting leadership. When we did demonstrate governing traits, we were likely labeled as "bossy." Being described as "bossy" by our teachers or our peers did not win friends or favor. Instead, we were more likely to have received negative feedback. As a result, we learned to shut down our authoritative side in our youth and instead choose the path of not just least resistance, but the path of rewards.

In their book *The Confidence Code: The Science and Art of Self-Assurance*, Katty Kay and Claire Shipman present an in-depth review of how women build confidence in their youth.[2] They report case studies of highly successful businesswomen, athletes, and women in the military that suggest confidence in women, or the ability to succeed as one's authentic self, does not come from thinking positive thoughts. Rather, a woman's confidence is foundationally shaped in us when we are children. Like most attributes, both genetics and life experiences affect it. Kay and Shipman proposed that even the most successful women can struggle with confidence due to social cues that were ingrained in us as obedient girls. They argue that to grow in confidence requires both taking action and taking risks.

Their conclusion regarding how confidence is shaped in childhood achievement by following a clear set of rules in both scholarship and sports made sense to me. When I read their book, a light went off in my mind. No wonder I felt disconnected early in my career between being my authentic self and being who others believed I should be.

My success throughout high school, college, medical school, and post-graduate training came by following a certain set of rules. However, once it was time for me to offer my ideas and exert influence in my work environment, those rules no longer applied.

Our obedience and compliance in our youth are rewarded. Staying in our lane early in our life allows us to be given responsibility and tasks. This path to success is reinforced as we earn stars, hear positive feedback, and are given more responsibility.

So why doesn't this work for us when we are adults? What changes? Shouldn't we be able to follow directions, stay obedient, and make our way to the top? If this is the footpath to getting what we want and where we want to go, why does obedience suddenly no longer work? Why are women overlooked for promotions, not chosen for roles despite demonstrating value, and not seen as viable options for frontrunners in new ventures, roles, and executive positions?

As we transition from obedient schoolgirls to career women, something changes. First, promotion, salary, and opportunities are subjectively given. No class syllabus, objective examinations, or rule books are available to follow to get to the top. Instead, we encounter negotiating, golf outings, and gender bias.

As a good friend, Deb Gilg, a retired U.S. Attorney, stated to me that oftentimes as women we follow the rules, keep our heads down, and deliver above and beyond what is necessary to try to get to the top. Then something happens to some of us. Deb describes it as a flip, a switch, a moment in her career when she decided to be her authentic self, no matter the risks.

For years Deb outworked all those around her in an effort to show she "belonged" in her male-dominated environment. She said no matter how sick or exhausted she was, she showed up, outpaced her colleagues, and did her best not to "outshine anyone." But one day, she realized enough was enough. She said, "If the men could be blunt and live to fight another day, so could I. I decided it was more important to be authentic than to be liked, so I said, 'You know what? This is me. Take it or leave it, this is who you're getting from now on.'" Deb said she later found out her nickname in the courtroom was "the smiling cobra." "I was always respectful," she said. "But that didn't mean I was afraid to strike when I needed to."

As Deb experienced in the middle of her successful law career, there will likely come a time in your career when you must assert yourself. With all eyes on you, you must say to yourself: *I am here. I can lead. I can excel. I can do this job. I am the best at this. Take me seriously.*

Flip the switch. The earlier you do this, the better. You don't need years of experience to figure out that you can take action, boldly share your ideas, or lead those around you. You may need some reassurance, definitely validation, and certainly some encouragement when you get beat up or knocked down. That's okay, and it's the purpose of *Between Grit and Grace*. My hope is that by the end of this book you will feel like the smiling cobra you are destined to be.

The Backlash Conundrum

It isn't easy to stand up, speak up, or assert ourselves in environments where we are normally quiet, compliant, and obedient. It's a departure from being amenable and waiting our turn, and these behaviors ingrained in us early on were further reinforced by the rewards we likely received from them. It also isn't easy to depart from this model when you know you will likely experience pushback, negative comments, or even hostile backlash.

"Coming out of the dugout" means risking being ostracized, laughed at, or shut down. There's research that backs up these experiences. Hannah Riley Bowles, who studies gender effects on negotiation at Harvard's Kennedy School of Government, has found that women who assert themselves during work-based negotiations are more likely to experience negative repercussions.[3] Both male and female supervisors are more likely to report negative evaluations of female employees who negotiate for their own interests and who display traits that are found to be more masculine, like advocating for oneself. Women who exhibit this behavior in the workplace face what the authors call "social backlash," or decreased likability.

But what happens when we stay silent instead of advocating for ourselves? Ironically, it doesn't necessarily mean we will be deemed as "likable" and experience positive evaluations. Research by Emily Amanatullah and Catherine Tinsley suggests the opposite: when women display non-assertive behavior and don't self-advocate, they also experience negative feedback, but in a different direction.[4] The backlash that less-assertive women experience is called the "leadership backlash."

In other words, data suggests that the internal conflict women perceive is real: there is a small margin of error for women in the workplace when it comes to negotiating or not negotiating, advocating or not advocating, demonstrating strong male or strong female traits. Assert yourself too much, and experience social backlash. Don't assert yourself when it is perceived you should, and experience leadership backlash.

A few years into my career as a junior physician, I became involved in three different medical societies to launch my national career. I started to watch a few women leaders in order to emulate how they navigated leading in a male-dominated profession. One senior woman was in charge of a high-ranking committee on which I was a junior member. I watched her lead the meeting with order and direction. She kept the meeting on pace, listened to those who had ideas, and steadily corralled members from getting off topic. I was impressed by her direct style of leadership and her no-nonsense approach to getting things done.

During a coffee break, I overheard two male members of the committee talking about her. "She's a real ballbuster, isn't she?" one said to the other. I remained quiet and tried to act nonchalant as I wanly smiled and stirred my coffee. "Can you imagine being married to her?" the other guy joked.

I felt sucker-punched. I didn't know her personally, but I respected her tremendously. She was one of the few women who led and she did it well, in my opinion. This is what they thought of one of the few strong woman leaders in our organization? I dismissed their comments and asked a male colleague, whom I knew well, his opinion. "She's good at leading; she's just not very friendly," he said.

I let those words marinate and thought about the men in leadership whom I respected and tried my best to emulate. They were direct, fair, good listeners, redirected conversations when needed, and kept the group on task and on topic.

Would I ever have called these men "friendly"? Would any of my colleagues use that term to describe them or measure their ability to lead?

I don't think so. I wouldn't. In my mind, they were good leaders, and I wanted to be like them. But I didn't describe them as friendly.

The message I received that day was clear: To be successful in the workplace, women must be both likable and unwavering. Possessing strong leadership traits is not enough; women must be friendly, or as the research above demonstrates, suffer social backlash.

I know what you are thinking: *Great! So what you're telling me, Sasha, is that the only way I'm going to find success is if I walk the fine line between being a ballbuster and baking cookies for the potluck? That I must perfectly navigate the fine margin between strength and approachability?*

Introducing the *Man*-ual

Actually, I encourage you to flip that mind-set. Like the switch attorney Deb Gilg experienced, flip it *now*. Yes, the research states we face a backlash when we demonstrate one trait more than the other; that is validation for what you may experience.

But this research should not define our next move. It shouldn't give us the road map for how to behave or provide what I call the "*man*-ual" for how we should react to society's norms. It should only bolster our ability to objectively say to ourselves "Ah, *that's* why that happened to me. It doesn't mean I am a failure, as I refuse to stay in the margins. It just means that being my authentic self is going to come at a cost."

The research previously mentioned revealed that men and women leaders with similar competence may be judged completely differently for their success. It allows both men and women to understand that gender biases are real. They do exist, and they are a part of our daily work environments.

But biases should not *stop* us from moving forward. If anything, they should *inspire* us. Before you think I've lost it and need a retreat, give me a few more pages of your time. I promise you, this change in mind-set is worth it.

The cost of social and leadership backlash you may face when you assert your skills and speak your voice in the workplace is real. *But so is your freedom and the internal peace you deserve.* Your leadership is an example to other women who come after you. It is an inspiration to those who stand next to you and wonder how they, too, can combine their skills with their own concoction of grace and moxie. When you crush societal expectations by acting, instead of reacting, to biases, *you champion change.*

You do this by being brave enough to be gritty, graceful, and authentic; risky, resilient, and real. Maybe you have identified with what I described and maybe you have experienced social and leadership backlash. Maybe you are wondering where to find the courage to lead authentically or why you should in the first place. Maybe you're feeling beat up, beat down, and exhausted from walking the tightrope. You are not alone.

You are normal. And the good news is, there are women just like you who have overcome similar obstacles placed in their way—and survived the backlash. There is truth in the stories of women who have risen above. When we hear their stories and incorporate their lessons into our experience, we all become more powerful.

PAMELA FINN IS A SUCCESSFUL ENTREPRENEUR AND business owner. She spent the majority of her thirty-year career working in the fashion industry where she was the first female line builder and buyer to work for Payless ShoeSource Inc. She built her company in an industry primarily manufacturing products for the sporting-goods industry. Pam was nearly always the only woman executive, as men ruled both the fashion and sporting-goods industries. Her work took her to China, where Pam describes walking into manufacturing companies that had never seen a blonde Western woman.

Pam is both fearless and brilliant. When I met with her for business advice, she told me that if I could imagine it, she has likely experienced it. At first glance, you would likely guess that Pam spends her days making cookies or shopping, as she doesn't "fit" the typical executive mold. She has beautiful eyes and a warm smile—but don't underestimate her.

Her advice to me was clear and direct. This woman has been through it and found success. She told me, "Sasha, you will be judged for being who you are, or you will be judged for being who others want you to be. So why not be yourself?" Pam says that women must find what drives them and be brave enough to pursue that drive even if it means standing alone. According to Pam, when you are brave enough to try new things and believe in yourself, others will believe in you, too. "If you are brave enough to take risks, you will surprise yourself," Pam says. According to the highly successful businesswoman and entrepreneur, we are far more resilient than we believe ourselves to be.

Coming Out of the Dugout to Support Other Women

The truth is, each of us will come to a point in our lives where we must decide to come out of the dugout. How we do it, when we do it, and why we do it will be different with varying outcomes for each of us. Our decision to assert ourselves, to advocate for ourselves, to negotiate, or to demonstrate male traits in the workplace does not mean that the next moment we aren't allowed to demonstrate feminine ones.

Another truth is that there are times in every woman's life that require us to be assertive. Whether it's in a professional or personal setting, I don't know a woman who hasn't had to advocate, assert, or negotiate for herself or others at some point. Whether or not society rewards us for the expression of those traits should be inconsequential. And while we know that's not the case and the backlash is real, we must keep on.

One of the most empowering antidotes to fighting gender biases is the social amplification of women supporting other women. There is quite a bit of recent discord on this topic, so let's dive in. Research shows that some women can be labeled as "Queen Bees": cold, isolating, and undermining to other women. Women also have gender bias of their own regarding how they relate to and view other women in the workplace. The phenomenon of women bosses being more likely to undermine other women, however, is unfounded. Important to remember as we view how women relate to one another in the workplace is that some amount of competition between coworkers is normal and can be positive.

Research by Leah Sheppard and Karl Aquino describes how male coworkers who compete with one another, or have workplace discourse, are more likely to be viewed positively and as having healthy competition in the workplace, while conflict between women is viewed by both men and women coworkers as having long-lasting negative effects.[5]

Marianne Cooper, a sociologist and gender researcher at Stanford University, describes the Queen Bee phenomenon as a result of an older generation of women professionals who found themselves isolated at the top levels of their craft.[6] In order to succeed in male-dominated environments, women at the top protected themselves from appearing "too female" by distancing themselves from other women. It's important to understand, according to Cooper, that the Queen Bee phenomenon is a *result* of existing societal biases.

Cooper says, "When men battle it out, they are seen as engaging in healthy competition and vigorous debate. When women do the same things, they are Mean Girls locked in a heated catfight." Why is this perception important? Have you ever heard a woman say, "I'm not like other women, I put my career first." Or "I identify more with guys than gals." Or better yet, "I'm more of a guy's gal. Women can be so mean." Sound familiar?

According to Cooper, women often learn to distance themselves from appearing to possess female traits. We don't want to appear to identify with other women in the workplace for fear of being labeled with negative feminine stereotypes. This "lack of gender solidarity," or distancing ourselves from other women, may be generational. While having some feminine traits, such as approachability, collaboration, and empathy, are seen as positive attributes, identifying with women as a "gal's gal" is not.

It's likely that all of us can think of a woman in our careers who has attributes of a Queen Bee, or we can recall a time when we have dissociated ourselves from other women in our work environments. I want to encourage you to think past your previous experiences with other women and consider what could happen if the reverse is true: there is power in the amplification of other women, and power is where real change begins.

Introducing the *Woman*-ual

What does that mean for us today? It means we write a new *man*-ual. We write something new by taking action. Let me introduce you to what I call the *woman*-ual. What does this look like? What does it include? It contains a litany of actions that will go against societal cues, normal human behavior, and unconscious bias. The *woman*-ual instructs us to

1) Affirm other women for their skills and achievements and not for their "likability";

2) Encourage other women who are at the top, even when they are labeled a Queen Bee;

3) Write, comment, speak, and repeat the achievements of women whose work we appreciate;

4) Elevate women publicly whose talents go unnoticed and whose accomplishments may not be recognized or compensated; and

5) Flip the switch and step into our voices, our strength, and our own version of leadership.

INTERNAL CHECK:

Stop for a moment and think about the previous list.

1) Grab a piece of paper and write down what you like about this list and also what makes you uncomfortable.

2) Think of the last time you reached out to a woman and gave her positive feedback. How did this make you feel? How did she react?

3) List three women you appreciate. Take the time to send each of them an email or note of affirmation.

As we become more authentic, as we dare to advocate for ourselves, we can also educate others by openly discussing gender biases and the backlash described previously with our male and female colleagues. For example, when I go into a negotiation, I openly state, "I'm going to negotiate for myself now, and as a woman, that likely means I may face some backlash. I think the best approach is to lay that on the table from the get-go." (I call this the bias-Taser approach, Sasha-style.)

INTERNAL CHECK:

Negotiation Tips

Negotiation can be challenging, as the cloud of likability is often sitting on one of your shoulders and whispering in your ear while success is on your other shoulder telling you something different. When I am negotiating, I tell myself I am showing myself self-respect. I give myself positive affirmations prior to negotiating, and I embrace my internal grit. I do the following when I go into a negotiation, which I also teach more in depth in the Brave Enough classes (see page 227 for more information):

1) Make a list of all the things you bring to the table, specifically, your value;

2) Make a list of what you need to continue bringing value to the organization or project. In other words, what are you specifically are asking for;

3) Last, and most important, list what you will deliver to the other party. In other words, what do they want from you?

As we allow ourselves to lead with grit, something magical happens. We gain confidence. If we act with confidence, it allows us simultaneously to give ourselves permission to show grace to others by supporting other women. Early in my career, I felt camaraderie with other women. I didn't recognize this until later, but it was likely due to the fact that there were more women at my rank and employment level. My superiors were mostly men, and I looked up to them to model their behavior. I watched them and learned what to do and what not to do as a leader.

As I advanced in my career, fewer and fewer women were in my meetings, on my committees, and involved in my national work with medical societies. Not only was I facing constant internal conflict from the fear of being labeled too strong or too soft, but also I felt increasingly isolated as I was often the only woman in my circles.

For several years, instead of reaching across the divide to women in other circles, I put my head down and worked. Not many women were around when it was time for me to present data, to pitch my ideas, and to work toward promotions. I felt more distance between me and the few other mid-career women who were also doing their best to stay in their lane and succeed in a male-dominated environment.

As you will read in this book, a pivotal point in my life occurred where I changed how I related to other women, not because I was smart enough to see I needed to, but because I felt as if I were floating in a sea alone, in need of a life raft. Standing on that raft were other women.

It took my being brave enough to reach out and grab hold of that life raft. I had to become vulnerable to other women. I had to admit to women, who may or may not have understood me, my shortcomings, my mistakes, and my struggles. I had to show other women my flaws, which were part of my true and authentic self. And it took a lot of grace, both extending it to myself and receiving it from others, to say, "Let's ditch the past and move forward."

Empowering other women and amplifying their voices didn't fix all the gender bias I faced in my career. But it did provide an enormous amount of relief for me: it normalized my experiences. It allowed me to establish a community of women to lean on, to bolster and push forward other women who were above me and behind me. It also allowed me to throw away the *man*-ual and start living my life according to my own *woman*-ual.

You know, the *man*-ual that says that once you're labeled a "ballbuster," your career will be lonely and isolated. Or that you can't negotiate for yourself one minute and show empathy to a colleague the next. The *man*-ual that says if you show masculine traits, you are harsh and cold, and if you show feminine traits, you are weak and not ready for leadership. The *man*-ual that says women do not support other women, and women disagreeing with other women are simply catfights between emotional individuals battling over silly issues. If you are a woman, you've likely read the *man*-ual, and you may be following it without even being aware.

In my opinion, the *man*-ual needs to be thrown into the trash. Flushed down the toilet. Placed in the sharps container. Pitch the *man*-ual. Pick up the *woman*-ual. As a friend replied to me once when I looked at her and said, *"Do I need Botox?"*

It's time.

CHECKING IN WITH YOURSELF   *Exercise 1*

After each chapter, I encourage you to stop reading and complete a brief exercise to allow yourself to do some internal work and write your own personal *woman*-ual. In the classes I teach and the Brave Enough courses I developed for women, I have found that time alone with ourselves to go inward is vital to personal growth. Grab a journal and jot down your answers to the following questions:

1) Think about a time when you "came out of the dugout." What made you decide to stand up, speak up, raise your hand, and assert yourself?

   _____

   _____

   _____

2) What was the outcome? How did you feel about it?

   _____

   _____

   _____

3) How did you process the reaction (negative or positive feedback) after standing strong? Think about how these experiences have influenced your ability to move toward your goals, and toward living authentically.

   _____

   _____

   _____

Chapter 2

Your Internal Voice: Frenemy vs. Fangirl

The most courageous act is still
to think for yourself.
Aloud.

— *Coco Chanel*[1]

Pick Me!

E arly in my career, I believed the world was mine. Hungry, inspired, and filled with energy, I worked hard, determined to succeed and emerge as a leader. I wasted no time. Writing, publishing, networking, and speaking; I did all the right things to show I had what it takes. When the first opportunity for a small leadership role came up, I looked to my right and my left and saw no one close to my level of productivity or experience. I was confident I would be picked. I wasn't.

Women enter the workforce equipped with the same skills, energy, and ambition to move up the ladder as men do. But time and again, we don't. Why? There are a lot of reasons, including some we can't control: biases, lack of sponsorship, an absence of mentorship, inflexible bosses, discrimination against women with young children at home—the list goes on.

In the previous chapter, we delved into some of the ways gender bias can play a role in the external obstruction women may face in their workplaces. Experiencing repeated backlash causes us to retreat. We start to question our abilities and wonder why we aren't chosen for the position that we worked hard to get. When we are overlooked, we ask why. Haven't we been following the rules, putting in the hours, and outworking those around us?

We can't control the external biases that affect us, but we can understand them and change our internal dialogue. In this chapter, I want us to focus on what we can control: our internal voice and what it speaks to us.

Another reason women don't advance as often as men do is one we *can* control: our confidence and our willingness to assert ourselves. Looking back at my first attempt to be tapped as a leader, I see my mistakes and why I was disappointed. I was quietly waiting for someone to notice all my hard work. I call it the silent "pick me!" syndrome.

If I had asserted myself and asked to be placed in that position, it is very likely I still may not have been chosen. But my disappointment would have not been reflected inward because I would have known that I did all I could do. I would have thrown a stone at the glass ceiling, and my ambition and qualifications would not have gone unnoticed. My frustration would have been externally focused, and it's an important distinction.

I *was* the most qualified candidate all those years ago, but looking back, I'm certain I didn't make it obvious that I wanted the job. I fell short by not being completely transparent and showing that I *desired* the job. If I had requested directly on paper that I planned on being a candidate and my experience and achievements objectively showed why I was qualified, then it would be transparent to all that the only reason I didn't get the job was that someone more qualified would have had to beat me, or it was simply due to bias.

Unfortunately, I handled this instance as if I were Sleeping Beauty waiting for her prince to come and wake her up. While I was doing the work, I wasn't requiring anyone to tell me *no*. As women, if we want to be chosen, we have to step forward. We have to *move* forward—and keep moving forward—until someone requires us to stop. We have to compel someone to tell us no instead of patiently waiting for someone to take notice and say yes.

As women, we often stay in the safe place of waiting to be picked, wishing for permission to step forward. We hold back on expressing our knowledge, even when we have the answer or the better idea in meetings. Afraid we might come across as "too much," we save our advice for the perfect time—which may or may not come along. Afraid of rejection, we don't place ourselves in the running for new roles or promotions, especially if we have stepped forward only to be overlooked in the past.

KATHRYN GLAS, MD, IS A PROFESSOR AND VICE-CHAIR IN THE department of anesthesiology at Emory University School of Medicine in Atlanta, Georgia. "While I rose up the leadership ranks for several years, I don't recall starting to have issues in my career advancement until I completed an MBA and started to be a threat to lead," she states. "It became apparent when I would suggest ideas to improve our workplace and my suggestions and requests were met with criticism and disdain. I persisted but was denied the role of division chief and told I lacked the national reputation required for the job. As is the case for many others, I was doing much of the work without getting due credit," Kathryn explains.

"I kept persisting to get credit for the leader I was being, until finally we had a change in leadership who leveled the playing field in the department. Though this helped me tremendously, when I myself became interim chair, I still struggled with being a woman in a leadership structure that was overwhelmingly male and was even told at one point that I was too assertive to be successful," she states. "Being on the receiving end of bias throughout my career has made me more aware and braver. I openly call out gender bias, and I train members of my department to understand their own biases to actively work to avoid biased decisions."

Why Not Me?

A year ago, I was listening to Hilary Blair, a professional voice instructor, speak to several hundred professional women. She posed this question to all of us: "How many of you have ever been called 'too' something?" She then asked us to complete the following sentence: "You are too *fill in the blank*."

The responses were a loud roar of "too bossy," "too emotional," "too direct," "too quiet," "too loud," "too sensitive," "too ambitious," "too harsh," and a dozen other adjectives. We looked at one another and smiled, realizing how common it was to be called "too much" of something. Remember the *man*-ual? It's likely if you step outside of the rules in the *man*-ual, you'll be called "too" something. This feedback is real and has long-term effects on our internal voices; it impacts our confidence.

An internal study by Hewlett-Packard, referenced in the book *Lean In* by Sheryl Sandberg, found that men apply for jobs even when they meet only 60 percent of the required qualifications.[2] Their female counterparts wait until they have 100 percent. A follow-up survey study conducted of both men and women, completed by Tara Mohr, dug deeper into reasons why women and men don't apply for jobs. She found similarities between the reasons, as both genders stated the most common reason was based on the belief they wouldn't be hired because they did not meet expectations.[3] The difference was that 15 percent of women said they were simply following the guidelines of who should apply, but only 8 percent of men responded with that answer, suggesting that, again, women are more likely to follow the rules. Women were also more likely to list being afraid of failure (22 percent) as a reason not to apply versus only 13 percent of men. Mohr says that women's fear of failure may be warranted, as she notes when women do fail, our failures are remembered longer and may have a more negative impact on our careers than our male counterparts.

These studies suggest that women get beat out for leadership positions by men who may not have more qualifications but who believe that the requirements listed in the hiring process are both optional and flexible. In the study, Mohr states, "Girls are strongly socialized to follow rules and in school are rewarded, again and again, for doing so. In part, girls' greater success in school (relative to boys) arguably can be attributed to their better rule following. Then in their careers, that rule-following habit has real costs, including when it comes to adhering to the guidelines about 'who should apply.'"

But why is it so hard for women to ask for things they want in the first place? Why is it difficult and scary for us to move forward, to throw our hat into the ring, and to say, "I want this. I deserve this, and I will get this unless you tell me no"?

Asking for an opportunity we want requires two things: the belief that we deserve it and the belief that we can do it. It takes both the action *and* the confidence to bounce back from rejection if we fail to get the job, the raise, or the chance. It is scary, it is energy taxing, and it is mentally exhausting. We often don't realize the emotional penalty we pay when we keep on pushing. I certainly didn't.

INTERNAL CHECK:

The Art of the Ask

1) Write in your journal something you would like to have professionally or personally that requires an ask.

2) Imagine yourself asking for this, be it a promotion, raise, time, or opportunity. List the feelings that come to mind when you imagine yourself asking.

3) List the reasons you are not currently asking for the opportunity. Are you waiting for someone to offer it to you? Why?

4) List the worst thing that would happen if the answer to your ask was no. What would happen to you if you heard no? What would you do?

> 5) Make a plan to make the ask. Talk about it with a close friend and set a date to do it.

After about a decade of kicking, scratching, and pushing my way forward, I remember the level of despair that came when I figured out that the higher I reached, the more exhausting it became. That my ability to keep bouncing up from being knocked down was getting easier in many ways, but the hits were bigger, and the price I paid higher. Shouldn't I face *less* obstruction as I climb farther up the ladder? What I experienced was quite the opposite.

And several times I became exhausted. Completely, 100 percent, running-on-fumes empty. It's important that I recognized those times and was transparent about the instances when I retreated, disengaged from the battle, and took a few months off to assess whether my approach was worth the expense. Why? Because so often we women take the path of least resistance, not because we aren't strong or smart enough to forge our own path, but because we are exhausted from forging it alone.

Intentionally Invisible

Sometimes we need a fuel break, and we need others around us to fill our tank. This is critical to say and to admit, so we can recognize this in ourselves and in one another. Stanford researchers have found an interesting phenomenon women face, which they call "intentional invisibility."[4] Dr. Swethaa Ballakrishnen and colleagues studied how professional women balance work and home life. They found that the majority of the women studied employed a "risk-averse, conflict-avoidance" strategy to navigate their work environments. They found that most women face biases both at home and at work, and they walk a fine line to keep up the professional status quo. They remain "invisible," aka behind the scenes, intentionally to avoid backlash. Unfortunately, this plays into gender biases and likely is enlarging, instead of narrowing, the gender gap.

According to their study, Ballakrishnen and colleagues state, "We find women across the organization reporting intentionally remaining behind the scenes in attempts to avoid backlash and maintain a professional status quo." The researchers went on to state, "While intentional invisibility allows women to successfully navigate gender unequal professional and personal landscapes, it could simultaneously present an additional challenge to career advancement."

In other words, who suffers? Women working below the potential of their abilities miss out—and so do our businesses. In its *Women Matter* report, McKinsey & Company studied gender influence in the top 101 companies worldwide and found that those with a higher proportion of women in top leadership scored higher in profitability, customer service, and seven other measures of organizational success. "At the microeconomic level, it is now regularly proven that gender diversity in management correlates with better organizational effectiveness and higher financial results," the McKinsey researchers state in the report.

I can identify with the research that states women are often "intentionally invisible." There have been times when I have been exhausted from fighting the good fight, and becoming invisible felt pretty good. Laying low and staying quiet felt like a much-needed reprieve. As a woman who is juggling many roles and responsibilities, I don't think there is any way we can go forward nonstop without becoming burned up or burned out at times. And we need to be able to say, "Friends, I need a little help; can you pick up the sword for a while?" But what we can't do is retreat for good.

We cannot give up and stay "intentionally invisible" forever. Why not? In the healthcare field, where women make up nearly 80 percent of the workforce, women hold fewer than 15 percent of top executive positions, which is better than most professions. Gender-based pay inequity exists at every level, across all occupations. I often hear women talk about the lack of maternity leave policies, pay gaps, and workplace harassment they face. Who do you think is going to change those things? Who do you think knows and understands the value, the challenges, and the issues surrounding gender equity the most? You and I, sister. You and I.

So, let's go inward and think about your internal voice. Let's figure out how to come back to the battlefield after the retreat. I'm going to show you how and tell you why it's worth the risk. For many women, stepping into new opportunities or leadership roles may present an internal conflict of having to be less of their authentic selves: less nurturing, less collaborative, and less passionate. They may struggle with the complexity of being both feminine and formidable. But strengthening our internal voice allows us to ditch the inner conflict between who we are to ourselves and who we are to others. If you think about it, the person you likely talk to the most is yourself. How many times have you heard someone speak about another woman, saying, "She should just be more confident!" or "She could do that, but she lacks confidence." As if confidence is something we can buy on Amazon or order an extra shot of in our morning cup.

Confidence in women is conflicting. Some evidence says the confidence gap between men and women is real, and the lack of confidence in women adds to the gender gap. Other data suggests we don't have a confidence problem as much as we have a bias problem. Studies also show that confident women face the "double bind," that women who are confident in the workplace are less likable, less likely to be hired, and more likely to be labeled as "difficult."[5]

Your Internal Fangirl

I can quote studies and data on either side, and we can argue for hours about nature versus nurture. But here is the thing: our confidence, as women, is most likely a combination of how we were raised, how we dealt with our past failures, our work culture, and also our ongoing ability to take action. Confidence, much like one's resilience, is *dynamic*. And it doesn't come by racking up achievements, it comes by taking *action*.

I know the data on biases, and I know how it feels to be rejected or passed over for opportunities you deserve. I also know I can't control anyone but myself. And let me tell you this: I am done caving to the expectations of the *man*-ual, and I encourage you to look inward, be brave, and take action. What does your *woman*-ual say? I encourage you to start writing it, sister. Put it down in words. Write your strengths, your goals, and your affirmations.

If you are doubting yourself, it is okay. You will change once you find your internal She-Ra. I did. I started listening to my internal fangirl and writing my own *woman*-ual. I realized it takes just as much energy to listen to my internal fangirl who tells me *I can* as it does to listen to my internal frenemy telling me *I cannot*.

See, your internal frenemy is really, really smart. She's Ivy League, speaks seven languages, and has a memory like no other. She remembers all your past failures and bad habits, and she's really good at reminding you of your limitations. She's a perfectionist, and her best friend is shame. It's easy to listen to her because she always knows the mood you're in—particularly when you are vulnerable—and she finds you just when you can't seem to ignore her.

Your inner fangirl, on the other hand, well, she's somewhat of an underdog. Psychology tells us that for every single negative interaction in our brains, we need about sixteen positive ones to overcome them, so your fangirl is constantly working out to combat your frenemy.

Your fangirl does CrossFit seven days a week just to have your back. She's trying to get your attention because she knows you really well. She has something your frenemy will never have: she not only sees you how you are, she also sees you for what she knows you can be. She's a visionary, and she's telling you, "Take a step forward. You are worthy; *you are enough*."

INTERNAL CHECK:

Changing Your Internal Voice

1) Let's take a moment to reframe our thinking, specifically when it comes to our internal voice. For example, think of a time when you have thought: *When I achieve X, then everyone will see how capable I am.* This is your frenemy talking, telling you your self-worth is dependent on your achievements.

2) Now reframe this action or risk you are facing from the lens of your fangirl. Write in your journal these affirmations based on your personal action plan:

    Taking this action will fuel my inner cheerleader and remind me of how capable I am because I am strong in these ways: (list)

    Taking this action will inspire other women to pursue their goals, even if I fail to achieve mine.

    Taking this action, no matter the outcome, will equal success to me because... (list)

The single most important action you can take is the first, small, deliberate step. Maybe it is a step to get back out on the field after a major career setback. Maybe it is a step into the gym after putting your health behind everyone else's in your life. Maybe it's a phone call that starts and ends with "I forgive you." Maybe it's letting the person who isn't your cheerleader go. Maybe it's a step out the door, knowing you aren't coming back. Maybe it's walking to the front of the room and saying: "I am qualified. Pick me."

Confidence: A Team Sport

One of the most awakening lessons I've had is that I can grow my own confidence when I elevate other women. You may be thinking, *What, Sasha? How does encouraging another woman to take action help develop and strengthen my internal voice?*

Confidence is not about being perfect. You don't cultivate confidence by perfecting your craft. You develop confidence when you amplify other women. That's right; women who amplify other women are more confident themselves! How cool is that? By helping others, you are more likely to grow your own inner voice that says, "You can do it, too!"

A recent study by Nick Huntington-Klein and Elaina Rose on West Point cadets found that having women in peer groups positively contributes to the likelihood that women will advance and stay in the field.[6] "We find that women do significantly better when placed in companies with women peers," the researchers state. "The addition of one woman peer reduces the gender progression gap by half," they noted. This study was important as it was randomized, which means there was less selection bias, and it was also performed in a male-dominated environment. They found that women cadets who had one other woman in their assigned peer group had a 55 percent chance of advancing to the next year and not leaving the program. However, if a woman was assigned to a peer group that had a higher number of women (six to nine), she had an 83 percent chance of remaining in the program.

ERICA HOWE, MD, IS AN ACADEMIC HOSPITALIST AND associate professor at the University of Kansas Medical Center. She also is the founder of the Women Physicians Wellness Conference. "When I decided to host my first conference exclusively for women physicians, I expected some negative comments from men who may have felt excluded, but I never thought I'd hear things like, 'What makes you qualified to host a conference?' from other women," said Erica. "After years of being overwhelmed and knowing other women physicians were experiencing the same struggles, I was shocked to receive backlash from women whom I was trying to help. I really struggled to understand why some of the women who needed my conference the most were also the most resistant to it," Erica explained.

"I had to come to terms with the fact that not everyone was going to like or support my mission. I just needed a core group of women to get into the car with me, turn up the radio, and drown out those critics," Erica said. "I started reaching out to women who were on board with my goals and focused on their words of support than any negativity that came my way. I had to come to an understanding with myself, too, that my message isn't right for every woman. I simply hope those women keep searching to find the support and inspiration they need in other women."

I read this as *confidence is contagious.* Just as it is important to encourage one another, it is equally, if not more, important to encourage yourself. Once I realized that listening to my inner voice had the ability to propel me just as much as it had the power to restrict me, I started taking notes. Literally, I started writing down my negative thoughts. Putting them on paper made me recognize how much I was listening to my frenemy, especially when it came to being assertive or advocating for myself. Even when it felt natural, and when I did advocate or negotiate or take charge, my frenemy would give me a play-by-play afterward and point out all the things I could have done, such as softened my tone here or been less firm there.

Ridiculous, huh? Then I also realized a tiny voice was cheering for me. She was in my corner, fixing my crown. She was telling me to go for it, to keep moving forward, and that no one was perfect, so why did I think I had to be? She encouraged me to lead, to assert my ideas, to state my opinions, and to take charge of situations directly because that's my style.

The Gift of Grace

Her voice grew, and guess what? So did my actions. One of the most important aspects of growing our confidence is letting go of our perfectionistic tendencies and showing ourselves grace. This is one of the most difficult things we can do because this requires us to let go of our failures and to throw off the labels that we and others often place on us, which we then start to believe about ourselves.

I can tell you that forgiving yourself is not just a one-time, aha, feel-good moment. It takes repeated work on your mind-set because guess what? You're human. I think we forget this sometimes. I do. I beat myself up for ways I could have spoken more articulately, led a meeting differently, or written something more eloquently. And when my professional performance isn't on my own personal hit list, I can always turn to my parenting skills or my appearance. Sound familiar?

When we give grace to ourselves, it allows us to increase our margin of failure. One of the most important aspects of increasing your confidence is to allow yourself a margin to fail. This may sound counterintuitive, but it is so important. Women tend to be more self-critical than men, and one study found that women tend to self-report their performance lower than men in the workplace.[7] Our own self-assessment and mind-set about how we perform can have significant professional or personal repercussions.

This is great news. Why? Because it reveals something we can change about ourselves, and *no one* else can take that from us. We can control our mind-set; we can give ourselves grace when we fall short. We can continue to push forward and advance in our careers, or we can pursue personal goals we set for ourselves, no matter what others write or say.

We have to know ourselves well enough to listen to our internal fangirl. Where do we begin?

One of the most thought-changing books I have ever read is the book *Mindset* by Dr. Carol Dweck. In her research as a psychologist who studies success, she found that the most successful people in business, technology, and sports were able to practice self-compassion and have what she calls a "growth mindset."[8] A growth mindset centers on the premise that it's not our talents or natural abilities we believe we were born with that lead to success; rather, it is our resilience, or our ability to bounce back after failures or setbacks.

INTERNAL CHECK:

The Power of **Yet**

One of the most powerful lessons I learned reading Dr. Dweck's work was the power of one word: *yet*. She reiterates the importance of teaching ourselves to adopt the word *yet*. For example:

We haven't received the grant we've spent years working on . . . yet.

We haven't gotten a pull-up . . . yet.

We haven't forgiven ourselves . . . yet.

We haven't received the promotion . . . yet.

We haven't passed the test . . . yet.

Of all the lessons in Dr. Dweck's research, this simple word has become so powerful to my ability to move forward. I challenge you to adopt this simple word and see how it changes your mindset.

Write down the three things you want to accomplish. Perhaps these are things you have tried to do but failed in the past. Reframe these thoughts using the word *yet*. Reflect on these statements. How does this change your future plans?

Woman, Know Thyself

While mentorship and sponsorship are important, we must know ourselves. We must know all the messy parts, the parts we want to shut off and keep closed. Building up our inner fangirl means we must do internal reflection to get outside results. I believe developing our confidence and listening to our inner fangirl is the bridge to authenticity.

Only you know what lives deep in your soul, the good and the bad. You are the keeper of the dreams that excite you, the passion that drives you, and the hurt that limits you. For years, I ignored what lived deep in the crevices of my heart and mind. It was like I was walking past a storage closet of boxes I didn't have the energy to unpack. As long as the door stayed shut, the rest of my house seemed to be in order.

Sometimes during those years, I would find myself with an extra hour I could spend by myself. Instead of being excited that I had been gifted time to sit and think, I was restless and stressed. I didn't want to go inward. In fact, that was the last thing I wanted to do. I wanted to keep the door shut. Going into the room was overwhelming. Where would I start? What box would I open first? I couldn't do it. So I left the door closed.

At some point, my life started to fall apart. I was forced to go into that storage closet. I had to open up each box, unpack it, and face the contents, both good and bad.

What I found in those boxes wasn't always warm and fuzzy. I found hurtful words from the past and labels placed on me by others. I found lies I believed about myself. I found failures and times when I fell short. I discovered hurtful things I did to others and painful words I had spoken to people I cared about. I found shame.

But I also found strength. The more boxes I unpacked, the easier it became to identify things I needed to throw away. I realized how much garbage I was keeping in the little crevices and tight places of my mind that didn't need to be there. Why was I holding on to these things? Why did I fear facing them?

When I finally gave myself the time to unpack the ugly, it made room for the beautiful things. I suddenly had room in that space to open up the boxes that held my stretch goals, the big dreams—those things I had been too afraid to state to anyone, including myself. What was hidden under layers of fear covered with years of walking the slim margin of being too bossy or too soft, was something I had kept buried for years: my *authenticity*.

Becoming my authentic self and developing my confidence didn't happen overnight. It didn't come to fruition after a couple of hours by myself with a cup of coffee. It took several years, and I can tell you I am still a work in progress. Just like you have to routinely clean out your home spaces, you have to do the same with your mind and heart. You have to give yourself time, on a routine basis, to go inward and unpack the boxes.

That is what I hope *Between Grit and Grace* does for you. As you read these words, I hope you are thinking of your own storage closet. Maybe you are considering which box really needs to be unpacked and sorted. Maybe you are thinking of that precious box full of your true hopes you have buried. Living authentically isn't an easy road. It takes confidence and self-awareness, both of which require going inward routinely. And let's face it, going inward for an hour or two is not nearly as appealing as pouring some pinot and turning on Netflix.

I wish I could tell you there was an easier way to grow your confidence and begin to own your abilities and voice. But the truth is, it takes a lot of grace and a lot of internal work. I wish I could tell you that once you speak up, throw your hat into the ring, and carry yourself as you know you were made to that all will fall into place and every challenge will go your way.

But here is the thing: you can do this. You can. I promise. The more you go inward, the easier it becomes. The more you listen to your internal fangirl and shut down your inner frenemy, the more you find yourself rising to the challenges life throws at you. The more you rise, the harder it becomes for those to hold you down. It doesn't mean all gender bias melts away, but it means that you keep rising, even in the face of it all. You become more resilient, more difficult to hold back, and more unlikely to keep silent.

Obstacles: A Good Thing

The more we rise and come into our authentic selves, the more obstacles we face. Why? Because we put ourselves into the fray and say, "Here

I am. I am worthy." We get rid of the junk in that closet, and we start to embrace our unique characteristics we have as women, which I believe God created. And we become brave enough to step forward.

The great thing that happens when we face obstacles is that we learn how to maneuver them. We learn how to go over, around, under, or through them. So the next time someone throws one in our way in the form of an underhanded comment or a biased evaluation, we can recognize it and know how to deal with it.

I want to encourage you, dear sister, right now, to put down this book. Grab a piece of paper and ask yourself which box in the storage closet of your mind needs to be cleaned out first. Give yourself grace and time to face it. Think of an hour this week when you can sit down alone, unplug, and identify your internal voice. Whose voice is the loudest? Your inner fangirl, or your inner frenemy? Where do the negative thoughts originate from, and are they true? Are they logical? Write them down, and then tear them up.

I am not saying that what you discover in the closet of your mind and heart will be easy. I am not saying it will make you feel good to go through each box. But I am saying that through the process, you will find *courage*.

And we need courage. A heck of a lot of it.

As author and researcher Dr. Brené Brown so eloquently wrote in her book *Dare to Lead*, "If you choose courage, you will absolutely know failure, disappointment, setback, even heartbreak. That's why we call it courage. That's why it's so rare."[9]

You are ready. You are prepared. Take heart. You are full of good things that need to be spoken, things that others in your workplaces and homes need to hear. You have the strength within you to face the hard things. Stop silently thinking, *Pick me!* Speak up and make your authentic voice heard.

Most likely your authentic self has a lot to say. She's been waiting to talk for a long time.

CHECKING IN WITH YOURSELF *Exercise 2*

Grab your journal and go inward. Take fifteen minutes to put yourself inside a room where you felt compelled to speak up, but held yourself back. Write down the answers to these questions:

1) Think of a time when you had an idea or an answer to a question but you stayed silent. Why didn't you speak up?

_____

_____

_____

2) What held you back from speaking up? Identify which reasons were driven by fear and which were driven by logic.

_____

_____

_____

3) Think about an upcoming event, meeting, or activity in which your voice may be helpful. Picture yourself speaking up or leading the discussion. What will you say? How will you feel?

_____

_____

_____

4) Visualize yourself as capable and knowledgeable and then write down how you will act.

_____

_____

_____

Chapter 3

One of the Boys… Not

There's nothing a man can do that I
can't do better and in heels.

—*Ginger Rogers*[1]

Choosing a Different Path

After years of hard work, I was beyond excited to be a finalist —and the only female in the mix—for a leadership position at a prestigious institution. It was not lost on me that a woman had never held that spot, but the same was true of most top jobs. I also had all the capabilities required, so when on the *last* interview day I questioned the feasibility of juggling motherhood and an executive-level role, I was surprised at myself. I had four children, ages fourteen, twelve, ten, and seven at the time. I struggled, thinking, *How would I make it to soccer games? Who would fix my daughter's hair for the dress rehearsal of her dance recital? How would I make it to curriculum night?* All of these thoughts swirled in my head, confirming the overarching thought: *This is why no woman has done this job. It cannot be done.*

I questioned the wisdom of my eagerness to take on such a demanding role. Was I being realistic? Would my obligations to my children present problems? Maybe there was a good reason only men had held this position. Then I doubted my ambition. I am *positive* if a woman had held that job prior to my interview, especially a woman with a family, I would not have been plagued by these thoughts.

During the final hour of the interview trip, I had to present my ideas for the job. I had to list all of the reasons why I would be the perfect fit. I stood up in front of the room filled with the committee and presented "The Best of Sasha." When I was done, one of the committee members asked me, "How will you balance all of the ideas you'd like to accomplish if chosen for this job with your role as a mother?"

I am not sure if that question would have been asked if I was a man with a family. I am fairly certain there are many who would say the question was not appropriate, but I also know it was likely what several members of the committee were thinking.

This wasn't the only time I faced this question in the workplace, but it was the first time I had faced it while interviewing for a major position at a large institution. I smiled and answered the question by stating I would do my best to balance both, be present, and then cited my many achievements as a reflection of my work ethic. I knew I was the only woman candidate for the job, and my likelihood at getting it was essentially zero based on previous statistics.

Internally, this question, however, did a lot of damage. This specific experience set off a downward spiral of self-doubt and thought distortions that took me a few years to remove from my internal beliefs. As the driver took me to the airport to head home, thoughts flooded in: *I can't do this job. If I take this job, I will be a terrible mother. There is a reason no other women were interviewed. I am not meant to take this job. I have reached my potential. I should be happy to stay in my current position. I will have to choose between my family and my job if I ever want to succeed at this level. This position belongs to a man.* I wasn't offered the job.

Internally, I was both relieved and sad. I was relieved because I didn't think the job was a good fit for me. I was a mom, and I didn't want to sacrifice being present in my children's lives. I was not sure if my level of energy and mojo would be a good fit at the executive level. I was passionate, and I was different from the other candidates... I was a woman.

I was sad because I thought I'd be really good at the job. I'm a strong leader who is a good collaborator, and I'm a visionary. I could have shown other women that top roles don't have to exclude leaders who happen to be mothers. I was different than the other candidates... I was a woman.

This entire experience, from the internal conflict after the interview to how I failed to get the job, tore at me internally for months. Why was I struggling with this? Why didn't I believe I could do the job? Why did I think being a good leader would mean I would have to be a bad parent? Wasn't I smarter than this? Wasn't this what I had worked toward for so many years, only to be simultaneously glad and sad I didn't score this top position?

Through this entire experience, I recognized an important lesson I want to share with you. I was looking at my abilities to fulfill the position through the lens of previous candidates. I was judging my abilities to fill the role in a way I would always come up short: by being a woman. I am not a man. And I never will be one. How had this happened? And if it happened to me, was it happening to other women?

The problem was, everyone else in that room had most likely thought the same thing. Due to unconscious, and likely some conscious, bias, the position was essentially created for a man. No woman had held it, and the question about my ability to do the job while balancing motherhood revealed the committee's concern about a woman serving in that role. The people in the room didn't want me to fail. They wanted the job to be successful. If the position was going to be held by a woman for the first time in history, maybe a woman with no children or with grown children would be a better candidate. Why? Because then she could fulfill the role similar to how it had been fulfilled in the past by a man.

INTERNAL CHECK:

You at Work and at Home

Grab your journal and take a few moments reflecting on the strengths you bring to your work and home environment. Answer these questions from your own viewpoint:

1) When you are working on a project with a team, what role do you most likely play? Discussion leader? Coach? Strategist? Organizer? Encourager? Communicator? Listener? Learner? Challenger? Recognize the value of the role you bring to the group.

2) Think about your role as a friend or family member. What specific strengths do you bring to your relationships? Encourager? Listener? Acts of kindness? Are you the one who makes everyone laugh? Loyalty? Accountability? Empathy? Recognize the value of the role you bring to your relationships.

3) How do these two roles differ from each other? Do they? Are they more similar or different? If they differ, do they cause you internal conflict? Why or why not?

Flipping the Script

Women experience an interesting phenomenon as they advance in their careers. When we look at those in leadership roles, we see mostly men. It's likely that our managers, directors, chiefs of divisions, our chairmen, and our vice presidents are men. The majority of our board members are men.

Our male role models, while often possessing great strengths, generally do not juggle the demands of work and family to the same degree that women do. These differences influence a woman's decision about standing up and asking for a promotion, even if it is not a conscious realization.

It certainly influenced mine. The essential truth I learned through this difficult challenge was that I had been measuring myself by a metric I could never reach—being a man. I was trying to emulate something I could never become, nor should I desire to. God made me a woman; instead of limiting myself in my own mind because I was not a man, I had to start accelerating myself internally because I was a woman!

The problem was, I had built a successful career for over a decade unaware I was trying to emulate and strive to achieve success as a man would. I had many great role models, but the majority in leadership with whom I worked day to day were men. I had measured the success of my attributes based on how similar they were to my male role models.

And the truth is, my leadership style, my communication style, and my problem-solving skills may or may not look like my male role models. My ability to collaborate, my tone of voice, and my writing may or may not sound like my male colleagues. I may possess some foundational characteristics of my male leaders, but they were just that: characteristics of being a good *leader*, not necessarily characteristics of being a *man*.

My choices, my work ethic, and my style were my own. And I had to start believing there was room for *all of me* at the top, not half of me, the half that was similar to my male colleagues, but *all of me*. The feminine attributes. The voice. The way I managed my time, even the way I dressed. *All of me*.

One of the most incredible things about human beings is that we are each completely unique. Essentially, billions of different women and men live on earth. Thus there are billions of versions of women, each unique with characteristics, strengths, likes, and dislikes. While patterns of traits differ between women and men, the expression of those traits is unique to a number of one. I love this.

Women, by nature, are strong group leaders. Whether extroverted or introverted, feminine or less feminine, women are team builders. We tend to listen to those around a table more than our male colleagues do, and thus when we lead, there is more innovation and idea sharing. Many of us are also more empathetic, which means we are able to perceive when individuals at work and home aren't engaged, and as such, we are more likely to collaborate and bring others to the table. We are more inclusive as managers, and as discussed in Chapter 2, this is why the most financially successful and innovative companies in the world have more women at the top, according to the research found in the McKinsey study.[2]

Now I look back at that interview experience, and I recognize how I let bias affect my response to the outcome. I may not have been able to control the outcome, but I could have responded differently. And I sure as heck would not have let it bother me for over a year. I am older now and a bit wiser, and if asked that same question today, I would answer differently. I would likely use my favorite response, which applies to most sexist or biased comments, "Can you repeat the question?" allowing for a pause and time for reflection in both the person asking the question and all who heard it. I would likely address the biased nature of the question right there and ask for further explanation of the question. And I certainly would not take the question to heart and convince myself I didn't deserve the job because I was a mother.

Losing Your Authentic Self…and Finding Her Again

I had to do some internal work: I had to reframe my mind around my character traits, my leadership style, and my success. I had to reframe my thought distortions, which had crept into my mind as a result of working in a male-dominated field.

I started to see all of the things I brought to the table: my collaboration style and ability to include others on projects, my ability to sponsor those around me without hesitation, my passion for encouraging others to reach their potential, and my relentless persistence to finish projects while maintaining a positive attitude.

Gallup research shows that organizations with men *and* women in leadership roles experience higher customer satisfaction scores, more innovation from employees and managers, and improved financial strength. Studies show women leaders score higher in "responsibility" to the organization, while men score higher in areas of "achievement," which suggests one reason why (according to a multitude of research studies) women excel in team building and collaboration. This sense of commitment to the whole group, more common in women, is often what makes us succeed as leaders. We have the data that demonstrates that a better balance between the sexes in leadership roles means the combination of unique male and female strengths, which can make a company more successful.[3]

Yet women make up only 30 percent of mid-level management. Women hold less than 10 percent of top-paying positions in the United States. This reality means it's more difficult for a woman not only to see herself in a leadership role but also to learn from women who've made it there. Most of our supervisors, managers, and executives are men. When we try to duplicate the leadership style of our male role models, we often find ourselves frustrated because it doesn't work. As a matter of fact, it backfires. Research shows that when women adopt behaviors that are considered "male" in the workplace, coworkers and supervisors judge them negatively, as we discussed in the previous chapter.

In an attempt to succeed, I believe we lose our unique female strengths.

To be taken seriously, we may walk, talk, and even dress like men. We lose our authentic selves in the process and become discouraged and disheartened. How do we find our way out of this double-whammy of identity struggle? First, we must figure out who we are. We must own our authenticity like we do our names. *Wait, who am I?*

A few years ago, I was in the midst of struggling to juggle motherhood and physician life, while being a wife, sister, friend, daughter…lots of things. A good day was when I showed up anywhere on time, in clothes that didn't have baby food on them, with hair that had been washed in the last week. Showering was my five minutes of oasis a day; if I could go from the shower to my closet without having to break up a fight, pick up a child, or wipe tears off someone's face I was *winning*.

I would look in the mirror and see a person staring back at me I didn't recognize. *What product can I buy to get rid of these dark circles? Is there a miracle drug that can put some pep back in my step? How do others look like cute moms who float from activity to activity in perfect leggings and matching boots while I look like I've been sleeping on a pallet in my garage? Why am I so tired? What is wrong with me? Am I dying? Is that grass in my hair?*

These thoughts were quickly interrupted by little people asking me for pancakes or telling me they swallowed a quarter. Or by text messages from work asking me for a consult. Or by emails blowing up my inbox asking me for a manuscript, inviting me to speak, or scolding me for forgetting to chart something in my anesthesia record at 3:00 AM. This was my life.

It's not that far-fetched, is it? I bet if you and I sat down and shared a pot of coffee (which, by the way, is my favorite thing to do with a new friend), you would share a similar story. You would likely tell me of a time in your life when you were a zombie woman, just going through the motions of work, home, and caring for everyone. Checking boxes. Afraid to go inward. Afraid to sit alone with yourself because you didn't want to face what's inside. Too tired to think about your interests or a hobby, let alone your passion, goals, or internal fire.

Or maybe you are in that space *now*. I know that place. It's lonely, and it's the last place you want to go to at the end of a long day. But, dear sister, here is the thing: *it is exactly where you need to go.* It is in that space where you start to uncover all of the layers upon layers of expectations that have been placed upon you by well-meaning people. It is here where you start to dig out of the hole of feeling inadequate, like you are failing on all fronts, and you aren't quite enough. It is in this space where you start the process of removing the measuring stick of success that you will never, ever reach.

INTERNAL CHECK:

Where Are You Quiz?

It is easy to lose our authentic self when we are trying to balance our many roles. We often take on responsibilities that require us to be something other than our true selves. Take a moment with your journal and write down answers to the following quiz:

1) List a job or role you are currently doing that you no longer desire to do. What is stopping you from removing this role or responsibility? Be honest with yourself as you reflect. What thoughts come to the surface?

2) Think forward to your calendar this month. Are any events or duties on your schedule that you are simply doing to check a box? What would happen if you said no to these?

3) What would it take for you to remove some of the things you listed above? Are you waiting for permission

> from someone else to remove them? Would eliminating
> unwanted responsibilities or roles cause internal conflict?

You have to be in this space and sit in it for a while to be able to understand your authentic self. Each of us has strengths, unique traits, and original ideas no one else can match. So often, however, we lose sight of our greatest strengths because of two main reasons: 1) we start down a path meant for someone else, and 2) we become so fatigued trying to overcome obstacles and walk in the narrow margin of that path, we simply have no energy to go a different direction.

If you find yourself there, be glad. That's right, get excited! Why? Because it likely means you are ready: ready to dive deep, ready to toss the layers and layers of expectations and feelings of inadequacy aside, and ready to get real. When I first began to share my own experience of being in this space with other women, I realized I regularly needed courage. I needed to be brave enough—a little dose of courage each day—to remove the expectations of others and figure out what leading my own life meant. I started my own company, Brave Enough, as a response to so many women telling me, "Sasha, I, too, am in that space, and I don't know how to get out of it."

The Path Back to You: Time with Yourself

Let's get started. I've read countless self-help books on leadership, *manuals* on how to get to the top, books on how to overcome difficult times, and studies on the science of pushing through obstacles. I've read books on self-discovery and authenticity. I've read books on how to get the corner office, how to love the skin you're in, how to lean every certain way to be seen.

Here's my take: The single most important step you can take to return to your authentic self—to confidently live the way you were created to live—is *time with yourself.* The single most important gift you can give others whom you love is an authentic, joyful you. That takes self-discovery and self-awareness. Both of those things take time—*alone.*

When we actually make routine, intentional time for ourselves, by ourselves, we give ourselves two things: space and grace. Space to delve into the areas where we perceive we are failing or feel like we are struggling. Space to uncover all the places we feel we are "too much" of something: too bossy, too quiet, too strong, too loud, or too emotional. Space to undergo an internal inventory: Why am I falling prey to other people's expectations of me? What makes me think I cannot be *all* of who I truly am?

Space and Grace

When we give ourselves this space, we allow ourselves to evaluate our feelings—both the good and the bad. We allow ourselves to write down our past mistakes and our future goals. We give ourselves permission to unpack, uncover, and undress the heavy things, the things we have been too afraid or too exhausted to unpack. It's okay if you are afraid. You are also extremely resilient, strong, and adaptable.

The second thing routine time alone with ourselves gives us is grace. Grace to pause. Grace to take a step toward forgiveness. Grace to allow ourselves to veer off the path we no longer want to be on, and grace to step toward our own authenticity.

Living as our authentic selves as women requires a lot of bravery and a whopping dose of grace. Why? Think about it: chances are that you are living not as yourself, and you are doing so successfully by other standards. What do I mean by that? You are doing your darnedest to please others. You are walking the path others want you to walk. You are trying to follow in another person's footsteps, and even if they are five sizes too big, you are going to do it or die trying. But when you expend your energy trying to meet others' expectations of yourself, you have no energy left to define your own. That's where grace comes in.

As women, we are often told to hide the very nature of who we are. We are collaborators, we are nurturers, and we are team builders. These traits require the ability to engage others, whether it's in intimate one-on-one settings or in larger groups. Women often possess the ability to engage others, and data shows that people who work for women bosses report higher engagement scores than those who work for male bosses.[4] Why? Women, in general, are good at reading others' emotions and engaging people in social constructs. We take time to find out what makes individuals excel and what they value. Women, in general, are natural includers; we score high in empathy when compared with men in strength assessments. Team building, empathy, and facilitating inclusion are not weaknesses. They are strengths. *Do you believe that?* Depending on the way you were raised, the way you have been treated in your workplaces, and your own internal thoughts, you may or may not.

When we reframe the thoughts around our individual strengths as women, we pretty much place dynamite on the road everyone expects us to travel, demonstrating we have another—a better—path to follow. We allow ourselves to show grit *and* grace and to travel the path we know we should travel—not the one everyone expects us to.

I think back to those years where I was in survival mode, and I can clearly see how routine time by myself would have been a lifeline. I was barely hanging on to my sanity, let alone doing any deep diving inside my soul. I didn't have a road map; I only had those who seemed to be succeeding in their life and work as my role models. Except none of them were in the same place in life I was, nor were they women. It took me a while to find my own path, and I can tell you that the single most important gift I gave myself was time alone.

Time alone allows you to see what your true goals are because it gives you time to understand your authentic self. Perhaps your goal is to pull back from job responsibilities and focus on your family or outside interests. That is perfectly acceptable, and it requires courage, bravery, and support to live your plan. Perhaps your plan is to advance in the workplace and not lose your family commitments while doing so. That also takes courage, bravery, and support because you may have to redefine what that role has looked like previously.

INTERNAL CHECK:

What Does Routine Time with Yourself Look Like?

Take the following quiz to determine how much time you spend alone nurturing your authentic self. Be honest as you reflect on how you spend your time.

1) When was the last time you took an uninterrupted hour alone without your phone, computer, or another person?

2) Do you ever avoid spending time with yourself? Why or why not?

3) Would you feel guilty if you were to spend an hour with yourself? Why or why not?

4) Think of your childhood. Did your mother spend time with herself? Did she model the importance of alone time? How did she go about self-care? What did her example teach you?

> 5) If you were to routinely spend time alone, what would you do? Where would you go to be alone? What time of day would this happen?

You may be thinking, *Wait, the most empowering thing I can do as a woman is to spend routine time by myself*? Yes. Away from your phone, your coworkers, your inbox, your family, and your children. Alone. Unplugged from the world around you and plugged into you.

To give myself time alone, I had to overcome two important thought distortions:

- *If I spend time alone working on myself, I am a selfish human being.*

And the next, somewhat harsh one:

- *If I spend time alone working on myself, I will uncover things I'm not strong enough to face right now, and I will feel worse than I already do.*

Whoa. Truth bombs, right? You may have read those two thoughts and felt like something sharp stabbed you in the gut. You may feel like skipping ahead to the next chapter…to the funny, easy-reading section. I challenge you, sister — don't.

You owe it to yourself to go inward. You owe it to yourself to face all the expectations you've allowed others to place on you and that you continue to do despite feeling inadequate and unfulfilled. You owe it to yourself to remove those things, one by one, by having honest conversations with others and saying no to things that you don't want to do.

You owe it to yourself and your loved ones to set healthy boundaries that allow you to give yourself routine time for self-care, and the space and grace to pursue the things you want to achieve in life. Boundaries that say no to what others want for you in order to say yes to the things you want for yourself.

You owe it to yourself to reframe your inner self-talk and how you visualize your strengths. You owe it to yourself, sister, to discover, list, and affirm your individual assets and passions, and let go of the viewing lenses you've accumulated from every person who's criticized you in the past.

You owe it to yourself to look at yourself through the lens of who created you, not through the eyes of your biggest critics. The ability to truly understand yourself, all the good and the bad, takes time. And yet, what is the one thing we seem to have so little of? What is the one thing we feel guilty taking for ourselves?

SHIVANI MUKKAMALA, MD, IS A PEDIATRIC anesthesiologist and assistant professor at Emory University School of Medicine and Children's Healthcare of Atlanta. She describes a time when she had to make a decision to change her internal monologue from a negative one to a positive one. "Due to complications during my pregnancy, after my daughter was born I had overwhelming thoughts that I was defective and a failure as a mother. I was in the midst of my intensive medical training and working demanding hours with a premature infant at home. My self-defeating thoughts seemed to be winning," Shivani explained.

"I started focusing on my positive attributes to drown out my internal frenemy. Each time I would start to feel inadequate, I would show self-compassion by focusing on a positive attribute about myself. At the same time, I started taking time for myself and caring for *me*. I began to take the time to look my best, and started working out by lifting weights to help my mind and body," Shivani said. "I also learned to ask for help. While it was a dark period in my life, I can see now that it taught me I was resilient, and I could resist the self-critic inside me saying I was not enough. As a result, I have learned to be stronger as a person and have become a more confident mother."

Success at the Expense of Authenticity

Our society likes to present awards and attention to the most tired women. We get an ego boost when we compare ourselves to others and find we are more overworked, more sleep deprived, and more frazzled than other women in our circles. We elevate women around us who rack up achievements and who seem to operate at a pace we can't compete with. We also misguidedly focus attention in the wrong direction. For instance:

- Instead of celebrating authenticity, we celebrate *succeeding*.
- Instead of celebrating self-care, we celebrate *overcommitment*.
- Instead of valuing relationships, we value *possessions*.
- Instead of defining our own version of success, we let others define it for us.

A pivotal moment came in my career when I had found significant success in a specific area of medicine. I was speaking ten to fifteen times a year on topics I could deliver in my sleep. I knew the material well, and I was getting so many invitations to write manuscripts, I couldn't keep up with all the requests. I had a research grant. I had national recognition. My hard work was paying off, and through persistent, diligent, hard work, I had made a professional reputation for myself as an expert in medicine. The problem was that at every step of success, two things were happening.

I was becoming less of myself, and I was also burning out. I had no idea how to stop either of these things. I didn't realize I could step back, that I had the power to say no.

After about eight years of nonstop working, I started "negotiating happy" with myself. I remember thinking, *If I speak on* that *stage, I will have succeeded*. I spoke on that stage; I didn't feel ultimate success. So I negotiated bigger. *If I am asked to author* that *chapter, I will have arrived. I will be satisfied in my career, people will respect me, and I will have succeeded*. I authored that chapter; the feeling of "check the box, you've done it" didn't come.

Okay, I thought. *If I am asked to write board questions for the national exam, that's it. That will be my ticket. I will have met my goals, and I will finally have the respect and the freedom to be authentically all that I am.* Guess what? I was nominated for the board; the feeling of freedom, the feeling of ultimately "reaching my goals" didn't come.

No amount of achievements made me feel like I had enough feathers in my cap to authentically be myself. No awards, publications, board memberships, or executive positions in national organizations validated my sense of self or gave me a permission slip to be me. *All of me.* No matter how much I achieved, I still came up empty.

Do you know what finally did? Coming to the difficult truth that the only person who was going to give me permission to live authentically was *me*. I had to stop assuming that if I racked up enough achievements and followed the path others expected me to follow, I would feel successful in life. I had to stop tiptoeing through my male-dominated work environment hoping I was following the right *man*-ual and not being too bossy, too domineering, too emotional, or too passionate. I had to start spending time alone with myself to identify what things I was accomplishing out of a motivation to please others or to feed my ego. I had to start recognizing the true, honest desires of my heart I was neglecting out of fear of failure.

I had to go inward, and when I did, I came to a very harsh, yet authentic, conclusion: I had not been living the life I was supposed to be living for a very, very long time.

I had been too afraid of disappointing nice people, and in doing so, I had responded "yes" to every ask for years. I had been saying "I'm sorry" to every critique and altering myself to each situation I was in to please all those around me. I had become a shell of the person I once thought I would become. In fact, I didn't even know who I was or how I would get back to her. Sound familiar?

Maybe you are reading this and you are feeling a little sucker-punched because you are *there*. You are in that very space of feeling suffocated by the weight of wearing layer upon layer of everyone else's expectations, buried and barely able to breathe. Your days are an accumulation of trying to catch balls others throw at you, and you can't seem to grasp them before they drop.

You are in survival mode. You don't have the energy to pause and evaluate because you are too tired. You hide behind the word *busy*; it's easier to say you are too busy to go inward than to sit and face the truth.

Let me encourage you, dear sister. You are not alone. I have been there, and I know what it is like to feel like a shell of yourself. I know what it is like to feel afraid to display your authenticity, to dare to shine as bright as you truly can, to be *all* of you.

There is space only you can fill. When you make the decision to find that space, you can't fit in it wearing the layers of expectations placed on you by others. There is not enough room in that space for the criticism you've heard from others, for your past mistakes, or for part of you. There's room only for all of you.

It is in that space where grit and grace live. In that space it's just you, your Creator, and all the unique traits, gifts, and talents that make you irrevocably *you*. My challenge to you is to go into that space. Open the door and sit. At first, you may not feel comfortable there. You are used to having a lot of different things to distract you. You may feel isolated, overwhelmed with thoughts, or completely exhausted. Hold on.

When we unplug and self-reflect in that space, something happens. We start to take our internal vital signs, so to speak. We begin to evaluate our current well-being. Why are we so tired? Why are we so isolated? Why are we so self-critical? Where did we pick up this jacket of insecurity, this scarf of shame, this oversized parka of need-to-please?

It is in this space that, we give ourselves grace. We start to remove, getting rid of all the things we've picked up along the way. Thoughts such as *Don't speak up in the meeting, you don't want to come across as a know-it-all.* We throw that thought into the trash and replace it with, *Gosh, I have a great idea. I will present it next time.* Or, *You had better just do that job without pay. As the only woman, you should be glad they chose you.* That goes into the rubbish pile as well and is replaced with *I am really glad they offered me the role. I will tell them I accept pending pay for the work I complete.* Or, *I can't cut back on my job responsibilities while my children are young because my professional reputation will never recover.* Switch that out with *I will write up a plan to show my employer how I can scale back while remaining productive and accountable.* When we give ourselves time to understand and know our true priorities, we can find the strength to live those priorities.

THE MORE WE UNDERSTAND WHO WE ARE AND LIVE OUR priorities, the more we can appreciate the journey toward our authentic selves. Sometimes it may come out of a dark place. Dr. Annahieta Kalantari is an emergency room physician and the Associate Residency Program Director at Milton S. Hershey Medical Center in Hershey,

Pennsylvania. "In my early career, I was faced with a tough choice of taking a stand to directly confront bias in the workplace. It was the right thing to do, but it was very difficult," Annahieta explained. "Rather than leaving the status quo, I decided to live authentically by speaking up. The backlash and retaliation were emotionally devastating.

"I overcame this hardship by reminding myself that this was a journey, be it a painful one, from which I would go on to learn many lessons. I've always wanted to be an independent, strong woman who didn't care what others thought. Though I may portray this image, the truth is, I have a ton of insecurities and do care what others say. This experience showed me that I must focus on the thoughts of the handful of people that really matter in my life and my own internal fortitude. Learning this really helped me get closer to the woman I've always wanted to be. This knowledge did help me develop my own definition of success rather than base my definition on the thoughts of others," Annahieta shared.

You start to remember the last time you pursued your passion and did something you truly love. It has been a long time, you remember. When was the last time you laughed so hard you had tears in your eyes? When was the last time you danced until 3:00 AM? When was the last time you could be you—*all* of you? These are the questions that surface in that space. You remember your grit, your strength, and your joy. You remember *her*.

The space between grit and grace is not a comfortable, easy place to be. It's full of tough questions and real answers. In that space, you can't hide behind your job, your boss, your kids, or your spouse. You can't disguise the real you behind others' criticisms or your past failures.

It's revealing and vulnerable in that space. It is also incredibly authentic, joyful, and freeing. I'm asking you to join me. Are you ready?

CHECKING IN WITH YOURSELF *Exercise 3*

Grab your journal, and reflect on the following questions. Write down your answers, and as you begin to spend routine time with yourself, think of how these answers may bring you closer to your authentic self.

1) If you were to describe your strongest attributes and character, what would those be? List them.

   _____

   _____

   _____

2) Think about which of your strengths you would identify as "feminine" and which as "masculine." Which ones do you feel most comfortable displaying in the workplace?

   _____

   _____

   _____

3) Do you possess certain strengths in your personal life that you do not embrace at work? Why?

   _____

   _____

   _____

Chapter 4

Everything to Everyone but Nothing to Myself

The most common way people give up
their power is by thinking they
don't have any.

—*Alice Walker, American author,*
The Color Purple[1]

When the Real You Shows Up

"**Y**ou, open the crash cart! I need you—*over there*—to get on the chest and start doing compressions. Can someone please hand me an 8.0 tube? Push epinephrine. Now. Again." The words flew out of my mouth—staccato—shortly after entering a patient's hospital room for a code blue. The room is tense, with tens of people packed into a cramped space, all doing specific tasks to help a dying patient. All waiting for a physician to show up and lead the crisis situation. As an anesthesiologist, I often run "codes," situations when a patient's life hangs by a thread and immediate medical intervention is required. Due to the sheer number of people in a room, it often takes me a few minutes just to navigate my way to the head of the patient's bed and assume the responsibility of the first step in saving someone's life: breathing.

While a group of nurses, pharmacists, resident physicians, respiratory therapists, and other hospital team members are ready to assist, it can be chaotic, loud, and obviously highly stressful. You don't have time for niceties. You must take charge and make sure everyone in the room hears your orders. For women doctors, this approach can come at the expense of significant judgment from the healthcare team. While male physicians gain respect by being assertive, the same gestures—taking charge and giving direct orders—can backfire for women physicians. We are judged for being firm, often labeled bossy, bitchy, or even rude. Years ago my reaction after a code would be "interpersonal cleanup" with the nurses and staff in the room. "Thanks for getting the crash cart so fast! Sorry if I sounded harsh," I would say on my way out the door after the patient was stable.

"Hey! How is your child doing in soccer?" I would ask the nurse cleaning up. I often said anything I could think of to make up for coming across as "too bossy." I finally stopped the "making nice" routine after realizing I had *never* seen *any* of my male colleagues do this. Why was I?

As a woman in medicine, I am often judged differently from a male doctor. When I take charge, give orders, ask for things, or direct people, my asks are taken much differently than when a male physician does. Research by VitalSmarts, a leadership training company, suggests that women who speak in an assertive manner in the workplace are judged 35 percent less competent when compared with men who use similar words, *and* they are paid an average of $15,000 less than their male colleagues, according to the study's authors Grenny and Maxfield.[2] "Speaking up in forceful, assertive ways is especially risky for women. An emotion-inequality effect punishes women more than men. Women are burdened with the assumption that they will conform to cultural stereotypes that typecast women as caring and nurturing. Speaking forcefully violates these cultural norms, and women are judged more harshly than men for the same degree of assertiveness," Grenny said.

It's the backlash for being a competent, direct, and assertive woman. In my job my patients are more important to me than any backlash I may receive for being confident and demanding in their care. However, it does not mean it doesn't hurt to know that I may suffer in evaluations and in my salary, not because I am direct and lead in my workplace, but because I am those things *as a woman*.

According to the study's authors, Joseph Grenny and David Maxfield, one way women can be assertive but decrease backlash is by using something they call "framing" statements. The authors give examples such as: "I'm going to express my opinion very directly; I'll be as specific as possible" before going into direct or assertive mode. While these framing statements, which serve to mitigate unconscious bias, are important, it is also worth recognizing that this is one more way women have to navigate around common biases just to get the job done. It is energy taxing.

I have a friend, Dr. Tiffany Love, who is a healthcare executive. She is a force: experienced, educated, collaborative, and a high achiever. Dr. Love serves thousands of people in her health system through her top leadership position as a minority woman. Tiffany states that not only is she the only woman in the board room at times, but also she is the only minority.

Dr. Love rose through the ranks because of her ability to connect with people, her education, and her work ethic. Being a high achiever and goal setter, she says that her career trajectory hit a boulder after an abrupt change in leadership. She had to work under a new chief executive who decided to silence her and destroy her confidence. "Overnight, my opinions, my expertise, my leadership, and my voice were not only wrong but no longer welcomed," Dr. Love said, describing her initial interactions with her new boss. "No matter how much I achieved, it was never enough. It became clear to me I could not 'win him over,' and my skills would not be valued under his leadership."

Dr. Love said that those years formed her and made her realize her worth. She also stated that those years serving under a leader who discriminated against her daily made her a better leader herself. Love, who serves on the faculty of the Harvard Women in Healthcare Leadership course, said that she has come to recognize the power of sharing these experiences with other women, to encourage them. "Women don't share their negative work experiences unless it's in private with a close friend. Successful women who find themselves in leadership positions often are too afraid to share their stories about harassment, discrimination, or times when we have been bullied in the executive suite." When she said this to me, her words resonated.

"I ACCEPTED THE DEPUTY CHIEF NURSING OFFICER POSITION because I was excited to work for a Chief Nursing Officer, my boss, who was a black woman. The Chief Executive Officer (CEO) of the hospital was a black woman, and the regional CEO was a black woman," Tiffany explained. "Statistically, this was a very unusual situation, and I was excited to have the opportunity to learn from women who had beat the odds and made it to the executive suite. At that time the organization was performing very well with respect to its quality metrics and budget," Tiffany stated.

"Several months after I arrived, there was a leadership upset, and the CEO announced her retirement. My boss informed me that she could not promise that she would stay. By the time a new CEO was selected, my boss had announced her retirement to begin on the day the new CEO arrived. I should have realized there was a reason she would leave on the first day the new CEO took office, but I was still naïve about executive suite politics. Two of the three women I chose to work for would be gone, and the third soon to follow," she stated.

"I found myself working for a man who immediately told me that I was not his choice to promote. He would not allow me to speak or ask questions at executive meetings where I was often the only woman in the board room. He verbally attacked my departments or leaders, and if I tried to speak, he held up his hand like a stop sign and said, 'I'm still talking.' I was essentially silenced in the board room. He scolded me in private for attempting to speak," Tiffany said.

"As a woman who was highly accomplished and celebrated, this was a shocking change for me. I had been encouraged to contribute my expertise when two women were in my chain of command. I was often my boss's designee to attend many executive-level meetings and encouraged to sit in and observe her leadership. Her inclusion encouraged me to work hard and exceed expectations.

"The environment change in the executive suite with the new CEO was obvious, not only to me but to other women in the room. I noted the CEO talked down to the women and put his hand up when women tried to speak in the board room. I did not observe him doing this to the men. He also seemed to treat the women of color more harshly than he treated white women; however, many of the white women verbalized to me in confidence their dissatisfaction with the way he treated them. He seemed to have a general disrespect and disregard for women, and it was evident in executive-level meetings," she stated.

"I built alliances with the women who had experienced the same treatment, and we shared information. I learned to control my outrage and to stand my ground. Living and working in the Deep South where racial injustice was accepted as a way of life, I learned to fight without anger but with skill and grace. I researched the laws that govern prohibited discrimination, and I found a way to gracefully identify violations of the law without stepping outside of the social norms of the executive suite. Staying silent was no longer an option, as I was determined to fight for justice for all of the women I had the opportunity to defend and speak up for with dignity and grace," Tiffany said.

Stepping Out of the Shadows

Like Dr. Love, I am a high achiever and an optimist. I don't like to share negative stories because I don't like to allow myself to think about negative experiences or to dwell on them. So why would I want to share them? When I sat down to map out the contents of *Between Grit and*

Grace, I had a bit of an internal war. *I want this book to be positive and uplifting*, I thought. *I don't want to drag anyone down, so I am not going to discuss the difficulties we face* was one argument I told myself. But on the other side of my brain, I had to talk about them. I had to normalize them and state them outright. *I have to share reality so we can awaken and write a new* woman-*ual* became my winning thought.

We have to step out of the shadows and share our truth. We have to be brave but not overwhelmingly brave, just brave enough. As I have traveled around the country and spoke to hundreds of women, I learned something critical: there is significance in describing the experiences we face as women. There is value to both men and women when we are vulnerable enough to open up and be honest with how we women must navigate our workplaces, our families, and our expertise. When we share our biggest struggles and our biggest challenges, we normalize what it means to be a woman. We step out of the shadows and find courage, hope, and solidarity. We also find the strength to say enough is enough.

At some point, we women come to the realization that walking the tight rope to be "just enough" for everyone is not working. When we hear that other women have experienced similar situations, we often recognize how much backlash we are facing in our own lives. We also realize how tired we are of trying to be everything to everyone and still coming up short.

But here is the most important revelation that so many women miss: we don't want to stop being everything to everyone. We may think we do, but we don't. Before you think that I've lost it, stay with me for a minute. I believe the reason most women continue to accept poor work environments, overcommit to everyone else, and refuse to stop placating others is because it's too tiring not to. We are *exhausted*. We are completely, 100 percent bone-dry burned out. We are empty. And it is easier to stay on the treadmill of pleasing others than to face our internal truths.

AMY SHAH, MD, IS A DOUBLE-BOARDED ALLERGIST,
immunologist, and wellness expert who lives in Phoenix, Arizona. "Early
in my career, I felt so different and so out of place. Besides being
one of two women in a group of thirty doctors, I was also the only
physician who wanted to participate in clinical research in nutrition
and wellness," Amy explained. "When one of my partners discouraged
me by telling me to 'concentrate on your patients in the office' and
not 'extracurricular activities,' I was disheartened for entertaining a
different career trajectory. As the minority, I felt like withering down into
my chair anytime I was at a board meeting. I didn't want to use my
voice or stand up for myself, and I faced constant criticism," Amy said.

"Soon it became clear that I had to exert myself or I would be
eternally unhappy. Creating an uncommon career path meant I had
no choice but to stand up for myself. I pursued a hybrid practice,
one with clinical work and wellness education. I spoke to one of my
biggest critics, the colleague who had previously dissuaded me, and
told him that this was my choice, I was helping so many people, and I
did not appreciate his comments. I was stern and firm. He was taken
aback," Amy said. "I stopped hiding my pursuits and talked about
them widely and loudly. I felt so free when I used my voice to confront
my colleague," Amy said. "Why did I need to hide or modify my life's
mission for someone else's comfort? I learned that I have a right to
take up space. I didn't need to become small every time I was around
a group of men, especially those who differ from me."

So we have an hour to ourselves? We self-soothe by binging on Netflix
or scrolling social media. We don't dare go inward. Thinking about our
authentic selves, thinking about all the things we want to do but can't

because we are overcommitted is exhausting. Thinking about our passions or a new hobby, are you kidding me? No way. We are too tired. Thoughts of being bold enough to try a new type of leadership, blaze a new trail, and lead as a woman? Nope. Too much pushback, too much friction.

Instead, we drink wine in yoga pants, answering emails at nine o'clock at night, and wondering how much more work we have to get done before we can crash into bed (*and please, God, don't let there be a toddler there. Wait, am I lying on a Goldfish cracker?*).

Intentional Giving Yourself Away

In 2009, Betsey Stevenson and Justin Wolfers published a study on the happiness of women in America. Using the General Social Survey data, they found that despite advances in salary, opportunities, and education, women reported experiencing less happiness in the 2000s than they did in the 1970s when compared with men.[3] "By many objective measures the lives of women in the United States have improved over the last thirty-five years, yet we show that measures of subjective well-being indicate that women's happiness has declined both absolutely and relative to men," the authors state. "These declines have continued and a new gender gap is emerging—one with higher subjective well-being for men," the researchers said in their report. While many obstructions for women in the workplace appear to be improving, our feeling of contentment is not. Why is this?

With every opportunity comes a choice to say yes or no. We feel pressure to succeed. We want to succeed, but we know that we must do it like a man, as the *man*-ual says. When we accept opportunities, they come with complex expectations and a list of must-dos that are foreign to our male colleagues. We can't lead as women without significant backlash. The internal conflict can lead to overwhelming fatigue.

We ask ourselves continually if it is worth it. At a pivotal point in my life, I realized that this constant stress of trying to please everyone, trying to lead as this hybrid she-man, had left me completely bare—exposed, weak, frustrated, angry, empty, and exhausted. I had become everything to everyone and nothing to myself. It was a moment when I realized I had said four words over and over to everyone but *me* for nearly a decade, if not more. And with those four words, I had intentionally given up my own authority, my own needs, my own passions, my *life*. "I can do that," I would say. "I will do it," I would repeat to a child, a colleague, a boss.

This was really, really hard to face. While I had hidden behind the guise of "I am so busy," the truth was quite the opposite. I realized that my overcommitment was intentional. I had become addicted to success, and achieving that came from my overcommitment. It was like a drug to me. It became normal to live in a constant state of stress and comfortable to say yes. Saying no felt harsh, difficult, and painful and provoked anxiety. Every single action, every promise, everything "yes" was intentional.

I had intentionally moved away from my authentic self. And this could only mean one thing: I had to intentionally move to get her back. For years I hid behind "I have to do this thing." The thing was either a job, a talk, a manuscript, a project, a commitment, or some other task. And I did them all like a robot. I didn't just finish them, *I conquered them.* All of them because I was a woman of my word. And it became ego-intoxicating despite also being completely depleting.

Deep in my soul, my authentic self would question me. Late at night, like a small child who wakes you, my thoughts would awaken me. And I always gave an excuse. *What about that girl's trip you promised you'd take this year with your friends? No, not this year. I have too many speaking engagements. Isn't this the month you promised you'd start writing for fun again? Maybe next year. When was the last time you sat on your couch and watched a movie with your family? It's just not the season for this.*

INTERNAL CHECK:

When Your Thoughts Awaken You

Often we can be chased by our internal voices that represent a conflict of self. It may be hard to distinguish whether these thoughts are positive or negative. Perhaps this internal conflict is good and is meant to lead us to a healthier, more honest version of ourselves. Grab your journal and answer these questions to help you determine if your thoughts are from your fangirl, trying to get your attention.

1) What are some things that your internal voice nudges you to do that start with "Haven't you always wanted to do _____ *(fill in the blank)*?" List them.

2) Why have you not pursued these actions? What reasons or obstructions are in your way?

3) Would taking these actions lead you to a more positive self? A healthier self? If so, write down how you could take the first step of action toward their completion.

4) Choose one of the items. Ask yourself what you would have to remove in your life (a current task, job, prior commitment) to accomplish the item on your list that is healthy, positive, or new.

What was really happening was an intentional giving away of myself. Like treat bags at a child's party, with each job, each task, each overcommitment, I gave away my time. Afterward, I saw a little more time for myself disappear. And piece by piece, someone would take it. The more I committed myself to others, the more comfortable I became operating with less of my own identity. Busy became comfortable, a way to numb and avoid any thought of going inside and dealing with my authentic self, which was starving.

And then a really dangerous thing started happening. My overcommitment became my shining star, a bright jewel I polished with each added task. "I don't know how you do everything you do," women would say. "Ask Shillcutt, she will get it done," colleagues would say. "I can do that," I would respond as I polished my magnificent halo of overcommitment and follow-through. *I'm a follow-through-er. No one can do this but me*, I whispered to myself. My ego puffed up. I felt accepted. I felt valued. I felt important. I felt seen. I was doing a good job following the *man*-ual. I was compliant and efficient and standing in the shadows, where it was safe.

I can see now that the only time I ever felt truly valued was when I received positive feedback for tasks I completed while being 100 percent overcommitted. I felt important when I delivered above and beyond what was necessary, doing projects I often lacked the inspiration to do. That, my sister, is called *sadness*. It is also an epidemic.

Power in the Pit

You may be reading this and thinking, *But that's not true, Sasha! Yes, I am tired. Yes, I am overwhelmed, yet I have no choice but to do all the things! I want to do less, but I have to do more. It's not that I want to, it's that I have to.* I challenge you right now to get real with yourself. It is not easy, and I understand it doesn't feel good. It's stressful to take responsibility for what feels like our biggest failure, our biggest mess. I have been there.

I am not coming to you from a pedestal of success. I am not preaching to you because I have *all* the answers and am perfect. If you think I have never stood in my pantry with five-day-old dirty hair, eating a sleeve of Oreos, crying my eyes out, you are mistaken. I am going to these deep places of self-discovery with you because I myself am there with you. I believe in women, and I believe getting real with ourselves is the key to unlocking our *might* and, simultaneously, our *peace*.

Here's the truth: you don't *have* to do anything. You choose to. The truth is:

- If you are overcommitted, you intentionally signed yourself up to be so;
- If you have lost your authentic self, you have given her away; and
- If you are empty, you have allowed yourself to be drained.

I know. You likely want to close this book, drop it into the trash, and go do the million things on your to-do list. It isn't easy to hear or accept these truths about ourselves. It is hard to accept that overcommitment and the situations in which we women often find ourselves—trying to please others—is a product of responding to an environment in the conventional way. The world is full of constant feedback that says to us, "This is what you do as a woman. You do what is necessary to be liked. You keep everyone happy. You feel valued by doing all the things. When someone asks you, say yes. You are a collaborative, kind, nurturing woman. This is your job."

But at the end of the day, we aren't happy. As the previous research described, we are not well. When we do things that do not align with our authentic selves and what we truly want to pursue, we become empty, busy, and drained. The constant overcommitment feeds our egos and provides a distraction for the things we may need to work on inside ourselves. We become a woman who changes hats all day long, trying to be the right coworker, the perfect leader, not too bossy but bossy enough, not too feminine but a little feminine. Trying to be the right person for everyone but ourselves often leads us to a place called burnout. Self-care falls by the wayside, as does the ability to lead our own lives.

If you can identify, and you are internally nodding, thinking, *This is me*, I am so glad. Why? Because here is the thing that is so good about being in this dark place of burnout: in the darkest of places, where you suddenly realize you have been intentionally giving yourself away, is where you find *hope*. It is in the gloomiest places where you can see the tiniest flicker of light. It is at the bottom of the pit where you are ready to grip that small but powerful light. You are ready to grasp it, hold on to it at all costs, and claw your way out.

It is in the darkest of pits where you are most determined to intentionally get your authenticity back. Maybe you are reading this and suddenly brimming with deep emotion. Maybe you are fighting tears and are feeling overwhelming regret. Maybe unexpectedly your internal frenemy has started whispering in your ear, *It is all your fault! You are to blame for your current state. You are to blame for your overcommitment. You are to blame for being completely exhausted, burned out, and off track. You are worthless. You are helpless. You are stuck.*

Hold on, dear sister. Tell your internal frenemy to take a hike. Take a moment and say these things to yourself:

- I am supposed to be here, in this exact place.
- I can and will reclaim my identity.
- I am wonderfully made.
- I will find her again.

I have learned many things on my journey to becoming more authentically Sasha. Through my work with Brave Enough, I have talked with many women from all over the world who are in the pit. In my courses, conferences, and classes, I have listened to their stories, heard their despair, and seen them rise like phoenixes from the ashes. Here is the thing: these women all started their journeys in the pit. Women who have found their authentic voices and embraced change did so when they were in the lowest of lows.

> *"And so,*
> *rock bottom*
> *became the solid foundation*
> *on which I built my life."*
>
> —J. K. Rowling, best-selling author

The women I have watched transform didn't decide to embrace their true selves while sitting at the top of the world, with perfect manicures, wearing their smallest size dresses, and rocking an amazing updo. They didn't dig deep into their internal selves when their bank accounts were stacked, their bosses had just voted them employee of the year, and their kids had earned perfect grades. These women didn't decide to change themselves when their relationships were perfect, their Instagram feeds matched their real-life home scenarios, and they could run thirteen miles without breaking a sweat. The women who have inspired me by being brave enough did so when they were at rock bottom, in the internal pit, and when they finally decided they'd had enough.

> *"Not until we are lost*
> *do we begin*
> *to understand ourselves."*
>
> —Henry David Thoreau

I can tell you, dear sister, that the times I have learned the most about myself are the times I have been in the pit, when I looked to my right and left and felt utter isolation, and when I felt lost, exhausted, and full of despair. Take heart, for once you see the flickering light of hope, you will realize you are not alone. Other women are in the pit with you. I believe that the most important being is also with you—the One who made you. And there are women who are holding the small match, ready to light yours.

> *"Remember, too, that sometimes*
> *'from our desolation*
> *only does the better life begin.'"*
>
> —William Shakespeare

The Steps Back to You

Are you ready? The thing about peeling back the layers of overcommitment and climbing out of the pit of burnout is recognizing that growing closer to the authentic you is a journey. Just as you need grit to climb out, you will also need grace to take a rest here and there. There is no expiration date on finding your authenticity. You won't suddenly locate your authentic self like a gala dress you've been searching for and say, *Aha! That's the one!* It's more like you're slowly and deliberately building a beautiful wardrobe of unique style that takes years of fine-tuning and that fits only you.

The first step to moving out of the pit and closer to your authenticity is to believe you are where you are supposed to be, that grace is in this space, as well as grit. Seriously ask yourself if you believe this, and stop the internal criticism for having fallen away from the true you. Beating yourself up over it isn't helpful, and it can only further delay taking back your self-authority.

The second step to your true self is to know you are exactly who you should be, to recognize you are a work in progress, and to understand there is joy in the journey. Yes, joy! Remember it? It may be a long time since you have given yourself permission to laugh at yourself, shown grace to yourself for the mistakes you've made, and accepted yourself. Self-work doesn't feel like work if you tell yourself that you can enjoy it. You don't have to suffer through saying no and removing things in your life that are holding you back. You can celebrate it!

The third step is to know you are not alone. The path you have traveled has been traveled by women before you and will be traveled by those coming behind you. This, to me, is the power of connection. It is the secret sauce to being comfortable and living your life according to your authentic self, not living according to everyone else's expectations. Women understand women. There is such power in the pack once you allow yourself to be vulnerable to a small group of women who love you *for* your honesty, not despite it. I have seen this through the Brave Enough community over and over. When we share our journeys and our struggles in authenticity, we find tips, tricks, encouragement, and support to continue on the path.

The fourth step is to forgive yourself. Yes. I challenge you to forgive yourself. You may be wondering, *What do I have to forgive myself for? After all, I've never killed anyone or even cheated on my taxes.* If you sit down with yourself, you may be surprised at what self-criticism you have on a repeating loop. Oftentimes, it is a few repetitive mistakes we convince ourselves we will always struggle with and never overcome that we beat ourselves up over. This is the most difficult work: to tell ourselves that we are okay and to accept self-compassion, which has far more power to propel us forward than does self-shame. Do you believe that? Let me convince you.

INTERNAL CHECK:

Do I Have To?

It is easy for us to think of all the times we have messed up and hurt others, but we often forget to forgive ourselves for the moments we hurt ourselves. Take out your journal and write down three self-behaviors or actions you struggle to forgive. Here are some ideas:

I struggle to forgive myself for all the times I said yes when I should have said no;

Ate, drank, or Netflixed away my emotions;

Berated myself for not being able to do it all;

Compared myself to the next woman, certain her life was more put together than mine;

Held back the answer, the idea, or the comment because I was afraid to speak up;

Hid my talents, afraid I would fail;

Told myself I wasn't smart enough, pretty enough, or fun enough;

Held myself to a higher standard than everyone else;

Questioned my ability to do the very job I am trained to do; or

Criticized my parenting skills, relationship skills, or friendship skills.

Kelly McGonigal, PhD, states in her book *The Willpower Instinct* that the motivation to change, or willpower, has more to do with how you see yourself and speak to yourself than it does with criticizing yourself.[4] "Self-compassion is far more effective than self-criticism and shame,"

McGonigal writes. If you think about it, shame is most closely tied to when we are in the pit because it is in those moments we feel as if we have failed ourselves. If we recognize that self-shame and criticism will rear its ugly head at the very instant we are most likely to desire change, we have immense power.

Shame: A Case Study

We have the ability in those moments to recognize self-shame for what it is: an opportunity for change. A desire to launch ourselves out of the pit; a longing to look for the tiny light of hope and move toward it. When we experience shame, we often get pulled into a negative cycle in which one self-criticizing thought (for example, *I am absent as a mother because I overcommitted myself*) signals a shameful thought (for example, *I am a bad mother*), which leads to a secondary negative behavior (for example, overindulging, overspending, avoiding interaction with our loved ones). This secondary behavior then feeds the original thought, creating a nega-tive, self-criticizing cycle.

For years after I had children, I struggled with finding time to exercise. I felt like if I left my kids any minute longer than already required to take care of my patients, I was being a terrible mother. I left the house each morning before they were awake and sometimes did not see them until the next day if I was working on call. How could I justify leaving them again to spend an hour at the gym?

Then I would think about how out of shape I was, which triggered feel-ings of worthlessness. That feeling of self-shame then initiated an unhealthy behavior: pouring myself a glass of wine. *I am already out of shape so what does a glass of wine matter?* Except it did. It mattered not because it was a glass of wine but because drinking it produced more self-critical thoughts. *I have no self-control. I am a bad parent and a worthless person.*

Yes. I spoke to myself like this. It makes me sad to think of how harsh I was to myself, how poorly I treated myself. I treated myself more cruelly with my thoughts than I have ever treated another human being. It took a friend (as it often does) to change my thinking pattern.

I was lamenting with my friend Ali over my nightly glass of self-shame-fueling pinot, and she said to me, "How about trying something to make you feel better when that thought pops up, instead of a glass of La Crema?"

"But I can't," I said. "I can't go to the gym that late. I have to get the kids in bed or pick them up from their activities," I moaned.

"Drop and do twenty burpees. Or take a ten-minute bath. Do something physical or kind for yourself, and make it your negative thought buster," she said.

I sighed. "Twenty burpees are not the same as working out."

She wasn't going to be put off by my excuses. "Just try it," she said.

This was a breakthrough for me. I realized something critical: When self-shame reared its ugly face in my head, it was an *opportunity*. An opportunity to *win*. And I don't know about you, sister, but I need to win sometimes. I realized that when I started down the path of self-criticism, I held the power. Pinot noir did not hold the power, I did. I would jump on that opportunity and do five to ten minutes of exercise, or take a bath, or sit by myself and just think. I stated affirmations to myself, poured myself a glass of sparkling water, and spoke kindly to myself. I often quoted Psalm 139:14 over and over in my head, as it brought me peace: "I am fearfully and wonderfully made." Oftentimes, this verse was the only thing I could think of because my mind was totally exhausted from work and kids. But it was enough.

Shame is a powerful feeling. As a deeply spiritual person with strong faith, I despise feeling shame. And yet I am often the person who self-shames and allows it to have power over me. Once I recognized that shame is a by-product of perfectionism, and is not a spiritual weapon to keep me on a straight path, I understood that shame was not from God. Shaming myself was not His desire for me. He created me, loves me, and wants me to be healthy. He wants me to forgive myself, and He wants me to have joy in my life. He created me for a unique purpose, and my struggles were just as important to Him as my successes.

When I recognized this negative, self-destructive cycle, and that it often came on my worst days, I was more prepared to alter its course, to change myself, beginning with my thought patterns. I was more likely to alter my behaviors and set healthy boundaries, which only boosted my confidence in myself. "I can keep promises to myself," I whispered and smiled. "I am a promise keeper to me!"

When you keep small, positive promises to yourself, it changes the way you see yourself. It prevents you from completely shutting down when that frenemy utters the tiniest whisper of self-shame or self-criticism. Keeping small promises to yourself allows you to practice self-compassion, to extend grace to yourself. It also allows you to develop *grit*.

Man, I have had a rough day, I would think at 9:00 PM on a Monday night. I'd been up at 4:30 AM, exercising before working a full day in the operating room. Off work at 5:00 PM, I ran kids to and from activities before landing at home exhausted. *Woohoo me! I did not self-sabotage! I am so proud of myself! I deserve some Sasha time so I don't burn out.* My new thoughts and a series of small, deliberate actions allowed me to grow in self-confidence. I was confident enough in myself to see that I didn't need to ask permission to begin to carve out space for myself. By extending myself *grace*, I started to grow in *grit*.

I had to recognize I was in the pit and accept that I was exactly where I was supposed to be. I had to understand that other women were with me, and I was not the only one facing these challenges. Even my friend Ali, who encouraged and challenged me to give myself grace, also shared her struggles. I had to identify that self-shame and self-criticism were in the pit with me, and I had to forgive myself. Then I had to *act*. Small deliberate actions. Not monster moves but just small steps that led to keeping promises to myself.

Then, and only then, did I truly start to become authentically me. I began to recognize that God had created me uniquely and bravely to live an authentic life. I realized that I didn't need success, overcommitment, constant ego boosting, or trying to please everyone. Most of all, I noticed that my two constant companions did not compete with each other but instead fueled each other. They were by my side through every step toward a better me: grit and grace.

> *"The more you approve of your own decisions,*
> *the less you need anyone else to."*
>
> —Dr. Mina Lee, surgeon

The Power of Gaps

DR. DANA CORRIEL IS AN INTERNIST WHO LIVES IN NEW York City with her husband and three boys. Nine years ago, Dana said she was drowning while grinding through the daily roles of her physician's life and mom's life. She took a good look at her life through a different lens and knew she needed something: a gap year. She recalls the decision to take what she calls was her "life-giving year that turned into three years." Dr. Corriel, who is back in practice and leads a group for physicians on social media, speaks all over the country about the power of taking time off to return to your work better.

Her reference to a gap year, the year many high school graduates take off to travel, discover their interests, and basically grow up before they enter college, was how Dana describes this time in her life. She said she discovered many powerful things about herself in this period as she took a break from medicine. Most important, she discovered her passions. She said it wasn't all sunshine and roses...but it was growth. It was intentional, and it was brave.

She found out that she loved art and antiques. She encountered joy in finding beauty in everyday objects, so she became a photographer. She had for many years struggled to be present with her children, but she realized during her gap that they were unchanged—the same kids when she worked as when she was at home: messy, beautiful, and real.

She talks about this gap year in the best of ways. Dr. Corriel says that if she had not been brave enough to take a step back from her job, she would not have discovered the many things that bring her joy, which she is now able to transmit to her patients.

Dr. Corriel encourages women to embrace the gap, which she says can be any period of time you take off to discover things you enjoy outside of your profession. It doesn't have to be a year. It can be a few weeks, a temporary shift to part time, or taking a few much-needed days off from your full-time gig. She states that when she went back into medicine after her three-year gap, she returned a changed person and physician. She was more present with her patients, more engaged on the home front, and more committed to joy in her everyday work.

When I listened to Dr. Corriel speak the first time, it struck me that we often have to hear permission from someone besides ourselves that it is perfectly acceptable to take a break from our work for a period of time. Isn't that interesting? Dr. Corriel presented data regarding professionals (in this study, primary care doctors) who underwent a "retreat" over the course of a year to strategically learn how to be more present and mindful in their lives. The result spoke to me: The doctors realized a lessened likelihood of burning out.[5] Intentional time away, or a gap, so to speak, may be what we need. Clarity often requires silence and spending time on a break away from the hustle and bustle of our demanding jobs, which often brings much-needed vision. I realized I needed to take a break, a few days to recharge. I needed a mini-gap year, and I was perfectly allowed to take one.

I could not drop everything and escape to the mountains and live in a cabin (although the thought of that filled me with momentary glee), but I could set some boundaries, take some time off, and regroup.

In order to live as authentic Sasha, the grace and the grit isn't a one-time vaccination. It's not like I get a dose of it and I'm immunized to all future breakdowns, challenges, burnout, or all-out mental Dumpster fires. I need continual gaps—routine mini-breaks—when I allow myself space and grace to evaluate where I am, where I am going, and who I am taking with me. I need to embrace the fact that I am imperfect, and there will be times when I need to rein in my life and reset my boundaries.

I also need these times of quiet, of pause, to realize that I am exactly who God made me to be. I can be gritty and take charge, and in the same vein, I can extend grace. I can be both collaborative and decisive. I can embrace being both a nurturer and a leader.

Isn't that what being a successful woman requires? Isn't that what we do day in and day out without even realizing it? Being unapologetically tough one minute and extending mercy the next? Why must we be judged for it, seek approval for it, or be under the microscope for being who we are made to be? When we stop running on the treadmill that others have put us on, when we pause to spend time alone with ourselves, we realize that we are made *imperfectly perfect*. We realize that we are *enough*. We realize that we are enough *as women*.

Ask yourself this: When was the last time I took a break and hit pause? When was the last time I stopped to evaluate how I am spending my time? Who am I trying to please? I challenge you, dear sister, to schedule a "gap." I encourage you to think about your life and how you spend your time. Find some white space in your upcoming weeks and months. Push pause and delve into you. My hope for you is that with each page you read, you give yourself permission to evaluate your life and your authenticity, that you allow yourself to be exactly the woman you were meant to be, with as much grit and grace as you desire.

At some point, to lead a successful authentic life, one in which you can be at peace with yourself, you must embrace the fact that you can be gritty *and* filled with grace. It's okay. We have permission to look like women, act like women, and *lead* as women. Let's do it. Unapologetically.

CHECKING IN WITH YOURSELF   *Exercise 4*

Do your actions match your authenticity?

1) Ask yourself if you have ever apologized for taking charge
   or being assertive when you knew it was appropriate.

   _____

   _____

   _____

2) Ask yourself why you apologized. Were you acting out
   of the norm for your usual actions, or were you acting
   authentically?

   _____

   _____

   _____

3) What expectations to act a certain way, if any, do you feel
   others have placed on you? List them. Do these expectations limit your authenticity or help you succeed? Do an
   internal check on how your actions compare with your
   authenticity.

   _____

   _____

   _____

Chapter 5

Brave Enough to Be Me

Do you remember who you were,
before the world told you
who you should be?

—*Danielle LaPorte,* Fearless Soul [1]

The Tipping Point

One cold Nebraska winter morning, well before dawn, as I dug around in my closet trying to dress for work without waking my family, I mindlessly grabbed a pair of stretchy black yoga pants and an oversized sweatshirt. Starting the day this way was my routine—I had done it for years—and the outfit was my normal attire (I would stash the clothes in my locker at the hospital within the next hour when I changed into scrubs for the day).

For some reason, that morning I paused long enough to glance at a cute skirt and pair of heels I hadn't worn in years. And as I did, I conjured a long-ago memory that had slipped my mind. As fleetingly as it had arrived, something snapped. I dropped to the floor and sobbed, overwhelmed by an unexpected sadness.

Why, despite all my achievements—happily married, mother of four beautiful children, board certified physician working in a noted medical center—was I so miserable? I was exhausted, and not by my schedule, but from the cumulative effect of failing to be true to my authentic self.

What am I doing? The uncomfortable truth enveloped me: I was hiding. I was standing in the shadows. It was safe there. It turns out, if you don't like the current version of yourself, stay in shadows. I didn't want to draw attention to myself, so I got up every day and wore mom clothes—clothing that came with this stage of life and that all the other moms I knew seemed to be wearing. That morning I didn't think I *deserved* to wear the clothes I loved, that made me feel good about myself. Or lipstick.

Over the course of seven years, I had given birth to four children, started and finished medical residency, began a new job as an attending physician, finished an executive fellowship, and took four sets of board exams. In the hurricane that was my life in those days, I lost myself. I lost my sense of self-worth. I stopped being brave. I stopped growing and learning. I stopped daring to be me, to step outside of the shadows.

Do not misunderstand. My job was great and I was succeeding at it. And I loved my kids more than anything. The issue with kids, like any blessing in life, is they have the potential to become your entire identity, self-worth, and measurement of success. They can take over your focus so that you ignore your spouse, your health, and your relationship with God. It is easy to do because your love for them is like a flame that grows stronger each year. And it's socially acceptable to make them your idols and your entire identity. In fact, as a woman, you are praised for it. "She is *such* a good mother!" we hear when we see moms sacrificing life and limb for their kids. "She puts her kids first!" we say when we describe the countless selfless acts we see another mother doing. We are *applauded* for walking around in sweatpants with dirty hair like zombie Uber drivers who just have one more kid to pick up and drop off before we can start packing lunches for the next day.

Second to my children, my career had become the measure of my self-worth. I had won a research grant, was earning national speaking engagements, possessed full clinical responsibilities...and I was fast approaching burnout. It was ironic. As the accolades, connections, and publications increased, I became increasingly empty. I had lost all resemblance to the real Sasha, and I wasn't sure how to get her back. It was like pieces of me had been chipped away, and what was left, although strong, wasn't a person I recognized. I kept waiting for someone to swoop in like a fairy godmother and redirect me or put me back together.

One day she came. I saw her in the mirror.

Go Ahead and Tip

Something broke loose in me that morning as I pulled on my sweatpants. I had no idea why, but it did. Some women describe it as reaching the end of the rope or having a midlife crisis or a wake-up call. For me, it was as if I had suddenly been placed in a giant, old-fashioned flour sifter. Slowly, God was turning the handle, and all the things that didn't belong in my life started to shake off of me. It wasn't comfortable, but it wasn't a crisis. It was purifying.

I was at the tipping point, and something inside me said, *Go ahead and tip.* All day at work I had this overwhelming sense of sadness. Deep grief settled over me for the person I had lost. At the end of my grieving, I was left with this truth: I had found success at the cost of my own authenticity.

Later that night when I returned home, I looked in the mirror and didn't recognize the person staring back at me. This person was exhausted, sad, out of shape, and pathetic—and I'm not talking about what I was wearing. Instead, this was the state of my being. I had become no one I recognized. I walked into my closet and collapsed in tears, again.

I spent the next two hours on the floor of my closet. I had some things to confess to God, things I had to get out. Years of building professional success had left me with little personal fulfillment. I had always attributed my ability to "bounce back" from failures or setbacks to my emotional intelligence. The fact was, in my quest for worldly success, I had become spiritually empty, and my emotional intelligence in the most important areas of my life—my spirituality, my family life, and my self-care—had all but shriveled to nothing.

I was hiding behind a successful career and my attempts to be a super zombie mom. I cried that night for the loss of myself, for the loss of the best Sasha, the true me. The true Sasha loved to take long walks and write.

I didn't remember the last time I had picked up my journal. The true Sasha used to play the guitar and loved having friends over for dinner. The true Sasha loved style and pretty shoes and traveling with her husband. The true Sasha loved having coffee with girlfriends and laughing until she couldn't breathe. I had robbed God, myself, and those I loved the most of the best of me. Dale Partridge, successful entrepreneur, says "Give your family your best, and your work your rest." For years I had completely flipped that. And now I was grieving deeply. Being in the sifter was necessary, and though I hesitated, I welcomed it.

INTERNAL CHECK:

The Sifter

Sometimes in life, we must be thrown into a sifter. You know, the one you grab when you are making cookies. Its purpose is to break down the flour, to refine it and remove impurities. It is not fun, but I have found that God will use an experience or trial as a sifter to reveal things in my life that need to go. During these times in the sifter, I had developed unhealthy habits. I was fostering an attachment to things like the praise of others. I needed to remove these things. In the sifter I have become aware of times I have failed as a leader, veered off the right track in my marriage, and become obsessed with my body image. While I'm far from perfect, I am grateful that God uses the sifter to purify me.

I challenge you to go inward and think about a time of challenge in your life. What did that period reveal to you? Did you learn things about yourself, such as realizing certain things were in your life that didn't belong there? Did you gain insight into any relationships that perhaps needed to be edited? Was there a negative habit or behavior that became transparent and thus it forced you to change? Are there currently attitudes, activities, and people in your life you are able to now see the need to be "sifted out"? Sharing these truths about ourselves with a friend often allows us to become brave enough to remove the things we know are holding us back from being our authentic selves.

Your True Spirit Is Calling

I've had a close relationship with God since I was a child. I've come to recognize that the closer I draw to God, the closer I am to my authentic self. The cool thing about God is I really didn't have to explain how far I had drifted away from Him; He already knew. He created me, and He was there for all my selfish, messed up, overcommitted, prideful, empty, and "successful" years. The ironic thing was that people were impressed at all I had accomplished in such a short time and at such a young age. My life looked perfect on paper. But the truth was, my brilliant resume came with a great cost, and the depth of that debt became clear to me that night in my closet.

The basis of who I am as a person is rooted deeply in who I believe God created me to be. To write a book about grace and grit—the two pillars of living authentically—and leave out my spirituality would be fraudulent. I have a strong sense of purpose that comes from my relationship with God and understanding who He created me to be. He doesn't make mistakes. It is His deep, unwavering love for me, despite my lack of faith in Him at times, that grounds me when all else around me seems to be shaking and moving in directions I can neither anticipate nor control.

Multiple studies have shown that attention to one's spiritual health is associated with positive mental and physical health. In a large analysis of research studies published on religion, spirituality, and health, most show that well-being, mental health, and physical health are increased in people who report being religious or spiritual. Investing and spending time on our spiritual health is crucial to living genuinely, particularly through life's challenges and stressors. If this thought resonates with you, great. If it doesn't, I encourage you to think about what spirituality is to you.

But First, Yoga Pants

First up, I had to start living authentically. And that started with acknowledging that I was not living as my best self, my best life. When we know we need to make changes, it's easy to become overwhelmed with how to begin. We tend to think that we need to completely re-create ourselves. We make huge resolutions and then fail because, at the end of the day, we are still lugging around the issues that got us into the mess in the first place. How many times have you said these words to yourself: *I am going to wear nicer clothes when I lose twenty pounds.* Or *I am going to take a vacation, or treat myself to a spa day, someday, when I have my life together and I'm more organized.* What you really want, what you desire, is self-care. You long to dress in a way that makes you feel more confident. You crave the ability to focus on your mental health and have time to exercise. You want to take a trip and relax and feel pampered. But you don't feel worthy because those things belong only to people who *have it all together.* And that is most definitely not you, right?

So you make a list of all the things you need to do to be a more "put together" person. What does "put together" even mean, by the way? It's like we think of ourselves as Humpty Dumpty, and once we find all the king's horses and all the king's men, we will suddenly find happiness, vacations, and skinny jeans that we can breathe in. So we make lists. Because we are good at lists.

- I am going to go to the gym every morning six days a week for ninety days.
- I am going to eat only vegetables, tilapia, and almond butter for six months. Then I will reach my goal weight and start wearing cute clothes again.
- I will go on dates with my husband or on girls' nights when I am fit, fun, and successful.
- I am going to purge my entire house and live according to an eraser board calendar and budget, completely clutter free and debt free. Then I can take a vacation and take care of myself.

Before you laugh, tell me you haven't had at least one of these thoughts. I call this erroneous thought process "putting our worthiness on hold." It took me a while to realize that the truth is, our happiness does not really change whether we are thirty pounds or three pounds away from our goal weight. Our worth does not increase if our house is in perfect order seven days a week and our checking account's fat. What matters is that you are moving in the right direction.

While we tend to focus on far-off goals, what actually matters most is *the very next step*. The small step you take, the one right in front of you, which is both feasible and obtainable. It is also the most important decision you will make. Not the one that appears to be 100 miles away, but the one that is directly at your feet, beckoning you to go in the right direction. When I realized that taking a small, purposeful step was all that mattered, I realized that I was meant to enjoy life *in the present*. Not when I had achieved a perfect body, not when I had earned a specific title or rank, not when I had it "put back together" again. I was surprised to enjoy being in the sifter. In it, little by little, the small imperfections sift away until what you are left with is the whole you, filled with good material.

I started with the basics. My first step was the small, simple task of dressing myself like I was worthy. I stopped waiting for perfection and started enjoying the process of burning away all that I was not intended to be, to rid myself of these heavy objects I had picked up on my way to becoming what the world told me I should be, what was expected of me. Instead, I focused on my true self, the one God had created me to be. My plan to wait to enjoy my life when I became the "perfect" version of myself was not only ridiculous but also kept me from taking the important next step. God never meant me to suffer through the metamorphosis; that was my choice. And I had been making too many wrong choices.

I gave myself permission to embrace and enjoy the process. I decided that step one, the very next step, was to dress *now* how I wanted to dress at my goal weight. It may sound superficial, but this step was huge for me. It was the beginning of my enjoying tipping over.

Don't get me wrong, there is nothing wrong with yoga pants. But they did not bring me joy. Nor did many of the things I was doing. As I did the things that brought me joy, I realized I had been putting them off, waiting until I had achieved some level of midlife stardom or achievement. That night I made a commitment to stop waiting, to stop living and working the way everyone expected me to, to stop going through the motions. It was time to be brave enough. I told myself a very simple truth and wrote it on a card that I placed on my bathroom mirror. I was:

- Worthy
- Enough
- Valued

- Unique
- Strong

It was time to change my mind-set. The results of those truths would follow. I threw away every pair of yoga pants I owned. I threw away sweatshirts and tunics and hoodies and every sad pair of leisure pants that filled my closet. I purged two-thirds of my clothing. The only apparel I had left were clothes I had been "saving"—for what? What was I waiting for? Someone to give me permission? A prize at the end of my thirties? *And the prize goes to Sasha Shillcutt for seven years of wearing black yoga pants, working overtime, putting herself last, and making everyone else happy!*

I started wearing beautiful shoes and lipstick and my "good" jewelry, all of which made me feel good about myself. I told myself that my outside actions were going to display the truths in my heart and in my head. I still remember the first time I wore high heels to work. One of my coworkers stopped me and asked if I was going somewhere after work, assuming I had a party or an event to attend. "What do you mean?" I asked him.

"Why do you look so nice? Who are you dressing up for?" he said.

"Myself," I answered. I smiled and I walked away. It was the truth. I was dressing up for me, and I felt so good, so authentically me, for doing so.

DR. R FOUND HERSELF IN THE MOST DIFFICULT YEAR OF HER life. She was at the end of her marriage, the mother of a young child, and going through major life changes. A friend added her to my social networking group, Style MD, made up of other women physicians. She said she never thought her life would have ended up the way it had, and she felt lost and lonely. As she read the encouraging posts from other women, she felt a flicker of hope.

One day she woke up and decided to put on makeup before work. When her daughter saw her that morning, wearing makeup for the first time in nearly two years, she said, "Mom! You are all better!" Dr. R broke into sobbing.

"Sometimes loneliness and shame can be so debilitating. The women encouraged me to take care of myself, and suddenly I felt I had a tribe of women behind me." She realized that one simple step—for her it was getting up early and committing to self-care—brought her hope and made her daughter feel the same. Often, the biggest thing you can do for yourself is to take a small step in the right direction—not a huge one, just a small one.

By the very simple act of dressing the way I really wanted to—authentically—I was respecting myself. I had spent a lifetime of keeping promises to everyone else except one very important person: me. This single step of wearing clothes that brought me joy was my opportunity to keep small yet valuable promises to myself. It was a simple promise to myself that held enormous power. By keeping a promise to Sasha, I was slowly investing in her. My life didn't change overnight, but this shift in thinking and behaving was the first step to living as my authentic self. I promoted myself to CEO of Sasha that day. In my company, we don't wear yoga pants to work. We save those for doing yoga and drinking coffee on the couch.

No More Lunch Maker

While I slowly worked on my exterior, the real work was going to be what I needed to address inside. Guess what? It turns out that sifting, as

I liked to call it, takes time. Time alone. Time to go inside. As women, our time is often not our own. In a study of over 1,000 physicians, female doctors who worked full time reported spending 8.5 more hours per week on household duties as compared with their male colleagues of similar rank and age.

Any whitespace in our week? We fill it up with tasks, duties, and work. It is rare for us to take time for ourselves, when we are free to be introspective, when we plan, relax, reflect, regroup, and reset. We can't move forward as women into our authentic selves unless we take the time to hear ourselves think.

So I decided to give myself an hour each day to work on becoming my best self. It may sound ludicrous. What woman has an hour a day to spend on herself? This focus on myself changed the way my husband and I interacted. At first, he was confused. "Are you wearing makeup and high heels to work?" he asked me, one morning, while I was getting ready in our bathroom.

"Yes," I answered.

"Why?" he asked.

I told him the truth. "Because it makes me feel more like the real me. I feel like I need to get back to who I really am."

Maybe it was because he hadn't had his coffee yet, but the weight of my words hadn't sunk in. He shrugged and kept brushing his teeth.

I got up early every morning and spent time on myself. Eventually, my husband took notice and told me how proud he was of me. "You seem happy again, babe," he would say. "You've always been beautiful, but you seem to be getting even more gorgeous. You are at peace."

I can't tell you how much this meant to me. The fact that he took notice of my self-care meant the world to me. That he didn't judge me for taking time for myself but supported me solidified my choice to make changes and set boundaries that would give me time alone. The change he saw in me opened up a portal for us to discuss our future and our personal goals, and to engage in authentic conversations.

DR. BRITTNEY TERRY, A PEDIATRICIAN WHO PRACTICES IN Tennessee, found that after having three children in six years, she had lost herself. She felt lonely and frumpy and was "barely a sliver of the girl I once knew. I had no time for myself, only time for my family and work. There was no working out, no friends, just my to-do list." Then she found her tribe.

Dr. Terry joined the networking group of women physicians I founded in 2015 and said she was suddenly inspired to make time for herself. She carved out an hour of her day for self-care. She started exercising, dressing with confidence, and has lost over sixty-five pounds. Dr. Terry didn't wait until she "met" her goal to inspire and encourage others; she did it all the way through. "I had forgotten how fun it was to spend time with my friends. I just kept working on myself, inspired by all the other women in the tribe who had overcome difficult life struggles, divorces, and losses. Because of this tribe, I am healthier and happier and a better wife and mother."

Did you know that one hour of your day is 4 percent of your total twenty-four hours? It's okay to invest 4 percent of your day in self-care, by yourself, working on yourself. *Becoming yourself.* The only hour I could come up with was from 5:00 to 6:00 in the morning. Sounds relaxing, doesn't it?

I got up at 4:30 in the morning and gave myself an hour to work on my authentic self. Sometimes I exercised. Other times I drank coffee and read Scripture. Sometimes I wrote in my journal. I took extra time to get ready, savoring every minute of alone time. Often I just thought. Planned. Dreamed. Now, before you think, *Wow, she makes it sound so easy*, let me be honest: whenever you decide to become brave enough to change your norm, it affects everyone else in your household, and that can be difficult. Women are often the center of their homes; as such, my decision to make one hour a day mine affected my entire family. It *was* difficult at first. For one thing, getting up that early meant I had to go to bed earlier, and it changed our entire family's schedule. I stopped making lunches at night because I barely had time to get through the nightly stack of school papers.

There was no more lunch maker. She was in bed. Asleep. My people were angry. But that was okay. They learned to make their own lunches, and it turned out that they were pretty good at it. My children all stepped up, pitched in, and participated. Prior to this, I had not asked them for help. I had thought that part of being a mother was doing everything. I was so wrong, and when I asked them for help with making lunches and organizing their papers, they stepped up. Did they do it perfectly? No. Did they clean up the kitchen the way I did? No. Was it good enough? Absolutely. Did I learn to let go of perfect and embrace brave? Yes!

When women take control of their lives and embrace being their own CEOs, they find power in saying no to others' expectations. But it's not without difficulty. I would be lying if I made it sound like it was as simple as making a cup of coffee. *Just find an hour, tell everyone you're unavailable, and forge ahead!*

One night after getting home around 9:00 PM from running kids to and fro, I announced that I was going to bed. My husband was just putting on his gym clothes to go to our basement and work out. He usually did this for an hour before showering and getting ready for bed. While he did his routine, my routine had been to run around the house, prepping for the next day, cleaning up and making lunches like a domestic Tasmanian devil, trying to get it all done so we could converse before bed sans kids. Then we'd spend twenty minutes talking about our day and exchanging business plans, aka child itineraries, for the next day before collapsing into bed at 10:30 or 11 o'clock, hoping to get a little sleep.

"Are you sick?" he asked, after I explained it was lights out for me.

"Nope," I responded.

He stood, a completely confused look on his face. It was as if I had announced I was dying my hair pink.

"I joined a gym. I am going to work out each morning before work, so I need to get up at 4:30 each morning. From now on, I need to be in bed at nine."

You could have heard a pin drop. He lumbered down the stairs, and I felt like I had told him I couldn't go to the prom with him. It's hard to disappoint those you love. But you know what? He supported me. It took a little adjustment, of changing our routines. In the end, he wanted me to be my authentic self. He wanted me to be my best self, and he knew I was taking small, important steps to change. He loved me despite the fact I was spinning a cocoon. And I thanked him, many times, for being so understanding and picking up the extra work that remained, as I no longer was doing it. I thanked him for being flexible enough to trust that the change in our little ecosystem, which likely affected him the most, would pay off dividends as I was becoming more of the person he fell in love with.

It Is Okay to Ask for Help

When you start putting yourself first, you will come up against resistance. Your family, your coworkers, and your friends are used to you saying yes. It takes a while for you to find your "no" voice. Most women are the ringmasters of their circuses. Everyone takes cues from us and expects us to be in the middle of the ring, orchestrating the madness, saying "yes" forever. When suddenly the center is empty for an hour, everyone is at a loss. And often angry.

Here's the thing. It takes grit to say no. It takes strength, fortitude, and major bravery. I get it. No, I cannot make your sandwiches anymore. I need to sleep so I can get up early and go to the gym while you are sleeping. No, I cannot run that errand. I need to do XYZ so that later I can spend time with my family. No, I cannot make that committee meeting. I have plans for self-care.

But here is the *big* thing I learned: instead of saying no, ask for help. My husband and children were completely willing to help me. I was the stumbling block. I was not letting them pitch in and help because I had my own guilt complex around it. I had to let that mom guilt go. I assigned tasks and hired a housekeeper. It was a huge investment for us, but it was so necessary and a decision I have never regretted.

When you say no, you are drawing a line in the sand. You are setting a boundary between others' expectations and your authentic, empowered, true self. These boundaries are so important, but they are made only by saying no. The truth is, when you set these boundaries, you disappoint nice people. That's hard.

While exercising most mornings, I felt like such a fraud for the first year. Every time I walked into the gym, I waited for someone to yell, "Hey, you! Over there! What do you think you are doing here?" I didn't think I belonged with all those fit people. Hilarious, right? But I showed up, regardless of my internal voice. I told my internal Negative Nelly to shut up and did ridiculous things like burpees and squat cleans, and, little by little, I felt stronger and more like me. The best me.

I realized something that year. Every day, to step toward my authentic self, I required two seemingly opposite things: grit and grace. I needed grit to say no to others, grit to ignore the voices in my head, and grit to get up each morning and take care of myself. But I also needed the exact opposite: grace. Every day. Grace to say yes to myself, and grace to give myself kindness when I came in last and felt like giving up or felt like a fraud. I needed grace for others who were angry about the new me. I had disappointed them. I needed both grit and grace to live authentically.

ACCORDING TO THE BUREAU OF LABOR STATISTICS,

American women spend on average 2.3 hours each day on household duties, compared with men who spend 1.4 hours on the same thing.[2] Women spend more time in meal planning, cleanup, childcare, and household management. Half of the women in the United States report doing daily food preparation in their homes versus 20 percent of men. While women have made large gains and comprise 47 percent of the United States workforce, according to the Bureau of Labor, women still carry the majority of household and childcare responsibilities. Seventy percent of women in the United States with children under the age of eighteen work outside the home, and 75 percent of them work full time. The challenge to carry both a full-time job and manage the household is a reality for the majority of women. When we add on responsibilities to care for children or aging parents (or both), often the first thing to go is our own self-care, which includes having meaningful friendships and relationships.

When we embrace masculine traits such as being formidable, fierce, relentless, and gritty, and we own them just as much as we own grace, we are able to live our authentic lives. When women embrace the fact that grit and grace complement each other and are not mutually exclusive, it enables us to lead our own lives. And guess what? When you live authentically, you find peace. And everyone who loves you notices, and it turns out peace is contagious.

Is Anybody There?

When I started working on myself, setting aside time for myself, and working on living as authentically as possible, something overwhelmed me. As I looked to my right and my left, I realized how alone I was.

Don't get me wrong. This book is not long enough to list all the amazing ways my husband fills my cup. To say he is my best friend is a gross understatement. He is my cheerleader, my sage, my comic relief, my masseuse, and my coach all in one. But there is a void in all of us that can be filled only by God, and I was missing Him. I felt alone and far away from God because I had made choices that had isolated me from not only Him but from my friends, who are an extension of God's love to us.

Ya Gotta Have Friends

I was lonely when I hit the tipping point. If I had to choose a word to describe how I felt, I could have used exhausted, broken, empty, flabby, weak, dejected. But that really wasn't the strongest word. It was *lonely*.

Have you ever felt lonely even though you are surrounded by people? Have you ever had a really rough day, or doubted yourself about something important, or just needed advice about anything from how to wear your hair to dealing with your mother-in-law? That's what women friendships are for. We need friendships with other women, mainly because they challenge us and pick us up when we fall. Why? Because they know how we fall because they fall, too.

We women wear masks. We cover each crack in our plaster with tapestries and pictures and perfect-looking wall coverings, so afraid that other women will see the truth: that we are human, and we don't have it all together. That we feel like frauds some days, that our kids ate cereal for dinner last night, that we haven't been on a date with our spouses in months, that we haven't been to the gym in six months, and that we didn't get the promotion. We are afraid to try because we are afraid to fail.

The truth is, when we let other women know the real us, an amazing thing happens. When we are brave enough to show our friends the real us, they fill a gap we didn't know existed. When we stop competing against and start encouraging one another, we realize that there is immense freedom in being vulnerable with one another. When we accept that we are worthy of being liked and loved even with our flaws, it allows us to accept others despite their flaws. More important, it allows us to accept ourselves. When we let ourselves be loved for our authentic, imperfect selves, we unleash bottled-up energy, creativity, and intelligence.

This is what true friendship looks like. And it is a beautiful thing. It is why I created Brave Enough, why I entertained the idea of women coming together to support one another through conferences and retreats, and why I share my story.

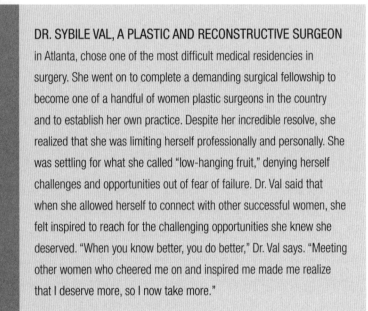

DR. SYBILE VAL, A PLASTIC AND RECONSTRUCTIVE SURGEON in Atlanta, chose one of the most difficult medical residencies in surgery. She went on to complete a demanding surgical fellowship to become one of a handful of women plastic surgeons in the country and to establish her own practice. Despite her incredible resolve, she realized that she was limiting herself professionally and personally. She was settling for what she called "low-hanging fruit," denying herself challenges and opportunities out of fear of failure. Dr. Val said that when she allowed herself to connect with other successful women, she felt inspired to reach for the challenging opportunities she knew she deserved. "When you know better, you do better," Dr. Val says. "Meeting other women who cheered me on and inspired me made me realize that I deserve more, so I now take more."

Scientific studies demonstrate how connecting with others routinely promotes emotional well-being. My friend, Ali, has two small children, a wonderful spouse, her dream home, and a successful career. A few years ago, she said that she thought she had it all. In reality, Ali felt quite the opposite. Internally she was unhappy, burned out, and exhausted.

She shared her dream with me. She admitted that it sounded crazy, but she dreamed of changing her job so she could be more present for her family. As her friend, I listened, told her she was capable of a major career change, and encouraged her to be open to pursue other opportunities. I honestly didn't tell Ali anything astounding. I simply listened to her heartfelt dreams—ones she had kept hidden. As her friend, I affirmed her as she had done for me in the past. I listened, affirmed, and encouraged.

Now, two years after sharing her dream with me, Ali works full time from home. She is thriving in her new work environment. She has balance in her life and is more confident than I've ever known her to be. Ali is journeying down her own new path. She will tell you that the power of friendship and being vulnerable to share her dreams with a close confidant gave her a brightly lit path toward achieving well-being and strength. She will tell you how being brave enough means taking small, deliberate steps each and every day to be the real you.

While it may seem completely unrealistic, we need friendships during the busiest times of our adulthood. When we are balancing work and family, while also building our careers, we are under a lot of pressure. It is in these times we need support from other women the most. Why? Because other women get it. Whether you realize it or not, if you look to either side of you, you will see women working just as hard as you are.

It is easy to let friendships go. Our lives are so busy, and too often we view friendships as "one more thing" we have to scratch off our lists. When your friend asks you ten times to meet for coffee and you say no because you feel guilty leaving your family when you aren't working like a machine, chances are there probably won't be an eleventh invitation. Without intending to, we let our friendships lapse. We think we can treat friendships like books: set it down and pick it up when we have time. We feel guilty when we spend time with our friends because societal norms say that in the business of our lives, a woman should care about two things: her family and her work. And friends, well, they are just for women who don't have either.

It turns out that when you find friends who accept you as your authentic self, it encourages you to be more authentic. And guess what else? It allows you to have *fun*. Remember fun? That thing you had in your teens and early twenties? Or once a year when you took a vacation? It turns out it is legal to have fun. In fact, we are supposed to have fun. When growing toward my authentic self, I gave myself permission to have fun.

I gave myself permission to enjoy things *as a woman*. I embraced style. I embraced my hobbies. I embraced red shoes and manicures and trips with my girlfriends and creative writing. I embraced date nights with my husband and laughing hysterically with my children and being the person God created me to be. I embraced my authority, my leadership, and my voice at work. My authenticity trickled down to every area of my life: work and home. I let myself be fully Sasha, and it felt so peaceful. I embraced *me*.

When was the last time you had a gut laugh? Having solid friendships is one of the most important predictors of possessing resiliency—of being able to bounce back from failure. Strong social support systems have been shown to be related to healthy aging, longevity, and a better quality of life. Nobel Prize–winner scientists Dr. Elizabeth Blackburn and Dr. Elissa Epel, in their book *The Telomere Effect*, describe how the length of telomeres (which shorten when cells age and divide) is affected by our social support systems during times of life stressors.[3] People who have deep and positive relationships have less cell death and longer telomeres. Not only do these people live longer, but they also have a better quality of life and are healthier. Having meaningful relationships strengthens our ability to overcome stress and difficult times, which we will inevitably face as we go through life.

If you want to live as your authentic self, you need to branch out, try new things. Move out of your comfort zone. Make your own path. Don't fret if along the way you stumble or fall. That's part of the journey. And you will need friends—brave friends, real friends—to help you back up.

Hard Is Normal

After I decided to go ahead and tip over, I started practicing self-care, made my friendships a priority, and altered my routine. I said yes to things

I wanted to pursue and no to things I didn't. It was extremely uncomfortable at times. Being authentic is at first. It's like setting off on a new exercise routine. Everything hurts before you feel better. And sometimes you wonder, *Why did I sign up for this?*

But then you get stronger, more flexible, and suddenly things that were hard before feel easy. Living authentically is similar. At first it hurts to breathe deep. You are using muscles you've never used, and it feels like everything is a struggle. But then you get stronger and movement is easier and everything fits better. You are finally becoming who you were meant to be. Life isn't perfect, but when trials hit, you feel comfortable attacking them as your authentic self, instead of doubting your response to every struggle that comes your way.

If you want to live as your authentic self, it takes grit. It takes formidable strength to say no to nice people, which is one of the most difficult things women must do while in the sifter. It isn't difficult to say no to people you don't respect or to say no to people who don't have your interests in mind. But to live authentically, you have to say yes to yourself and no to what others want you to do. When you live as your authentic self, you find power and peace in being who you are. It requires tapping into your grit. But that's okay because we are accustomed to doing hard things.

Hard is normal.

CHECKING IN WITH YOURSELF *Exercise 5*

What's Your Tipping Point?

Grab your journal and complete the following exercise:

1) Identify something you want to do but have not done because you think you need to achieve a personal goal before you would deserve it.

_____

_____

_____

2) Write down one thing you want to do but you've been putting off until you are more "put together."

_____

_____

_____

3) List the steps required to get you to the end goal.

_____

_____

_____

4) Then think about the very first step. What can you do to take that first step? Don't focus on the end goal. Focus on this one small step. What is stopping you from taking it?

_____

_____

_____

5) Meet with a friend, someone who truly cares about your best interests. Confide in this friend that you are going to take this first step. Examples: making an appointment for a personal trainer, hiring a life coach, taking a dance class, purging all your old clothes, signing up for a leadership class.

_____

_____

_____

6) Take the first step. Then treat yourself! Reward yourself for the *most important* step—the very next one!

_____

_____

_____

Chapter 6

Be Bossy; It's Okay

You've always had the power, my dear.
You just had to learn it for yourself.

—*Glinda, The Wizard of Oz*[1]

The Art of Leading Authentically

s the Chief Executive Officer (CEO) Emeritus of Tufts Medical Center, Ellen Zane is a bit of an anomaly. She's one of the most successful women in health care and currently serves or has served on nine corporate boards across the country. During her time at Tufts Medical Center, she transformed it from a struggling hospital system, which was the product of a failed merger in the early 2000s (in one of the country's most competitive healthcare environments), to one of the nation's most stable institutions.

Earlier in her career, while in her forties, she had taken on the role of CEO of a municipally owned community hospital—that had only eight days of cash on hand. In both the Tufts Medical Center and community hospital experiences, she struggled with how much she should tell employees, who, she learned, were largely in the dark regarding the dire situation of their employers. Should she reveal the truth about the financial insecurity of the system and risk losing hundreds of nurses and other staff, or keep quiet and let folks continue to work in ignorance of the near-bankrupt status of the organization that provided their paychecks?

She chose to do the former. When I met Ellen at a conference where she was speaking to executive leaders, she talked about how hard it was to tell people there would be cuts in some departments and why preservation of cash was vital to the organizations' futures. She had to explain there would be a moratorium on many purchasing requests, and there would be few new hires, even to fill positions vacated by retirement, until the system was financially secure. She was in her dream job but during a difficult, unstable time. She couldn't win people over by simply telling them what they wanted to hear. She had to be honest. She had to be the leader she was hired to be.

Ellen's decades of success in a difficult field were built on her willingness to be honest, strong, and authentic. Her role required her to be direct, focused, and "bossy" at times. Her success grew as she cared more about utilizing her authentic skills to make critical decisions in a competitive environment than worrying about how she would be perceived by those under her direction. She understood that leadership is not always a popularity contest.

Ellen endured some difficult times when she faced harsh criticism. During her day instructing us at the conference, she said that there were times when she entered the hospital and it felt like an eternity walking down the long corridor to her office. She admitted instances of feeling as though she was constantly looking over her shoulder, waiting for someone to launch a grenade at her. She admitted to experiencing loneliness, but two truths comforted her: knowing she was doing what was right for the medical center and what was right for its patients.

I have thought of Ellen several times throughout the last few years. When you hear a story of a woman who has gone through the fire and come out the other side wiser and with resolve and wit, you think: *I can do this, too. I can live and lead as me.*

You also learn that these trials make you who you are. I like to think of them as both short and long workouts for one's identity. Who are you? It's as if trials and hardships whisper to you, "Let's go through this workout and test your level of fitness." Only in this case, you aren't testing your heart rate or how far or fast you can run. You are testing an entirely different level of your DNA—who you are at your very core. Who are you emotionally and spiritually when you have to take a stand? Do you become more like you or less like you? Do you say and do whatever it takes to fit in, to please others? Or do you emerge more like your authentic, gritty self?

The Likability List

During my year in the desert, when I was struggling with my self-identity and burnout as a result of trying to be "just enough" for the people I did life with, I dove into the literature. I read leadership books, women empowerment books, and self-help books galore. I devoured books on happiness, on understanding your personality, and on teamwork. (Feel free to laugh, but at my core, I'm a scientist. When I have a problem, I read. A lot.)

I took notes from each book and scribbled advice from each author into my journal. My notebook was full of snippets of the author's advice like: "Speak last if you're in a meeting—your word will linger." Or "Be direct, but follow it with compassion." And "Women who have a balance of both masculine and feminine traits make better leaders and get higher scores on evaluations." And my favorite: "Lean in, but not too far; you'll get your head whacked."

After a year of studying how I should live, how I should lead, and how I should project myself in my culture, I felt like I had personality whiplash. The accumulated laundry list of do this and don't do that and change this about yourself felt like an impossible list to follow. I was wiser and knew what the leaders thought, but I was no more authentic than before I read advice from the experts.

I tried following the list. I really did. I attempted to be and act in a way that would make everyone happy, including me, by bringing me more success and likability. But then something struck me: Isn't following a likability list the very thing that made me burn out in the first place? Isn't that why I am in this year of the desert because I am empty from giving myself away, from walking the tightrope of being too masculine or too feminine?

So the answer to bouncing back from my overachieving, people-pleasing life crash was to be *more* people pleasing?! Hold on. Wait up. That's the moment I said, "Enough is enough." I realized then that I needed to throw the rules into the trash. It may seem as if I'm being rebellious with my "No, thank you" to all the advice coming to me from years of evidence and study.

You are correct. I am saying no. Those who know me aren't surprised, for I'm an Enneagram Type 8, aka the Challenger. It's who I am, and let me tell you, being an 8 in a woman's body is tiring. Downright exhausting at times. Sometimes I find myself in the fetal position thinking, *Can't someone else do the fighting today?* I am here to tell you to throw out the rules of "How to Be Successful as a Woman." Chuck them. Rip the pages out of your journals and notebooks and delete them from your phone.

The truth is, the more you embrace being *you*—loud, quiet, firm, compassionate, direct, loving, collaborative, boss-lady, or whatever mix of traits that make you unique—you *will* be successful as you define it. You can be both grace giving and gritty. You can be who you are, and you can lead that way. Will you face obstruction? Absolutely. Will you confuse people? Yes. Will you receive social backlash? Heck, yes. Will you become so comfortable with it that you let it roll off your back? Yes. Can I get an amen? And another? *Amen!*

> *"And the day came*
> *when the risk to remain*
> *tight in a bud*
> *was more painful*
> *than the risk it took*
> *to blossom."*
>
> —Anaïs Nin

What Is Your Worth?

When we women are fighting to advance in our careers, when we are doing our best to live authentically, we must face the uncomfortable truth that being bossy isn't how we made friends as young girls. We didn't earn gold stars in class by telling everyone around us what to do, and we certainly didn't become the teacher's pet by taking charge. As discussed in previous chapters, studies show that women are judged negatively for being assertive and authoritative in the workplace. We often face backlash when we employ our expertise over others in critical situations. Data also shows that when women in leadership positions make mistakes, they are judged more harshly than men who make similar mistakes.

What this data says to us is this: we have to accept the fact that we will encounter internal and external conflict when we live our lives authentically as women. Externally, people won't always understand why we set boundaries or take charge when we are the most qualified to do so. Internally, we will likely struggle occasionally, wondering if we are too much of this or too little of that. It takes courage just to show up every day as *you*. It takes what I teach women in my courses—being *brave enough* for the day—to show up authentically being who you are *as a woman* with the courage to get through your daily tasks.

That's okay. It's a sign of growth, of flexing our wings, of showing up as all of us, not part, but whole. I'm not advocating conflict, and I'm not telling you to just suck it up, sister. But I am telling you that when I am 100 percent Sasha, I often face a stiffening of sorts, not all the time, but sometimes, by those who so desperately want me to follow the *man*-ual they have made for countless women who stood in the spot before me. Or maybe my authenticity makes them uncomfortable because it causes them to briefly reflect on their own sense of identity. The point is, it doesn't really matter. You will face backlash. The more authentically you live, the more backlash you will face. The good news is, the less it will bother you.

When I come up against backlash, I know that it's probably a sign that I am being myself: honest, truthful, and direct. I view it as an indication that I am growing, and I perceive it as a *good thing*. When I am facing significant backlash for being authentic, for taking a stand or asserting myself, all I need to do is remain. If I can look at myself in the mirror and not find fault in my intent or my actions, I know I am to stand. Not take a step forward, not explain myself and take a step back, but just stand. Unwavering, unflinching, just standing. When facing giants, sometimes standing is enough.

AIMEE LOWE IS A BUSINESS ATTORNEY IN OMAHA, Nebraska. "As an attorney, most of my days require taking a stand. In the world of litigation, until the court renders its opinion or the parties mutually agree on the dotted line, there is always resistance from the opposing side. Every day I advise on risk, and if the plane can't clear the runway, we push back. Sometimes the adversary is on my side," Aimee explained.

"I've had to go under fire and silence a senior partner who sabotaged a deal, refuse a client's demand to file an unwarranted ethics complaint against opposing counsel, stand in the gap on behalf of fellow employees and colleagues who required defense, stop a trial midway through after discovering a multimillion dollar accountant's error, and refuse to bill a client who had no money to put food on the table," Aimee said.

"The best way to overcome any pushback is to expect it. Do your research, be nimble, and know your essentials. It's okay to have resistance—women shouldn't equate it to failure. Resistance simply means the other side also has something to say, but you hold the keys to approval or denial," she said. "If you are willing to do the research, cross-examine yourself, and walk all the way around the problem, you will not only know what you need, you can honestly evaluate the opposition's position. Give on the nonessentials; hold firm on the essentials. When it's time to walk, be ready to walk."

What keeps us standing in the face of giants who are trying to conform us into the litany of actions our culture or society says women are supposed to be, do, and say to be liked, accepted, and promoted? We have to understand the root of our *worth*. Whoa. Yes. Your worth. I'm not talking about confidence, but your worth and who you believe yourself to be. For me, I identify myself as a child of God. I know at the very core of my being, I was uniquely created with a combination of characteristics and ideas no one else has, or will have, in the entire history of womankind. How cool is that?

It is the very basis of how I perceive my significance. No action or inaction, no failure, no mistake, no label, no word written about me in an evaluation, and no title can add to or subtract from my worth. My value was given to me by the One who created me to be uniquely, innovatively Sasha. And I believe it is the same for you. There is only one you. Only one person who can lead and live in your space with your talents and characteristics and the lethal combination of grit, grace, ideas, and lip gloss.

When we understand and believe that our worth as women is not defined by someone else, we recognize we have it in us to be gritty and to extend grace. We can be wholly significant and working on ourselves at the same time. Read that again. *We can be completely valued and worthy, just as we are, while simultaneously improving ourselves.*

I remember the first time I actually realized that who I am—all of the messy parts of me—was not supposed to be defined by someone who held bigger titles, made more money, or was a size smaller than me. This truth convicted me because for years I felt my worth was tied to specific actions, like working harder than everyone else and delivering more and more. I waited years for some fairy godmother to bless me from above with a lifetime supply of dry shampoo, relaxing massages, and an hour a day to myself. Bless me. She wasn't coming.

It took me years to understand I wasn't supposed to measure myself against societal norms or what a terrific book or amazing speaker told me I was supposed to be. I realized that for me to live and lead authentically, I had to get really comfortable with this fact: My success isn't measured by my current "feeling of worthiness" because my worthiness is not tied to my own success. My worth is something untouchable and unchanged by my own actions or anyone else's.

When I embraced this truth, I also realized that no one can measure my success but me because no one knows what success looks like for me except one person: Sasha. I define success as living authentically. This is my personal measure of how I am doing. Have I connected with those around me whom I am doing life with, or have I spent my free time on social media today? Am I more concerned today with my looks or with my heart? Have I spent time today getting real with myself about the messy stuff deep down, or have I numbed the thoughts that bubble up with three vanilla scones? (Nothing against vanilla scones; I'm 100 percent convinced that when I get to heaven there will be a bottomless pot of steaming hot black coffee and a tray of vanilla scones that never runs out.)

You can't measure success on a piece of paper or with a title because success to us, as women, comes from recognizing our worth and then doing our best to accept that we can't alter it. So how do we begin to do this? Once we understand our worth, our value, we then can accept that living authentically means going against societal norms. We understand that leading authentically means others may judge us and not like us, and we are okay with that.

Why are we okay with that? Because others' judgments do not change our worth. We understand that living authentically means disappointing nice people who desperately want us to be something we are not. You may be thinking, *But, Sasha, I don't want to be a leader. I have no desire to advance in my career. Let someone else do it.* Hear me out, dear sister.

A Leader of One

You cannot live an authentic life unless you embrace the fact that you have to lead *yourself*. Until you are ready to stop hiding, to stop trying to disappear but instead come into your own sense of identity, you won't be able to set healthy boundaries and live your life according to how you define success. That requires leading *you*.

What is leading? It is not holding a title. It isn't only for those with power or intense drive or a fast-paced career and an overwhelming desire to launch to the top. It is important to lead authentically because most women I know are leading *something*—if not in their workplaces or departments, they are leading in their homes, their schools, their communities. Some of the most authentic women I know don't lead lives following the title and path of someone else; in fact, they often do the opposite.

They are innovators who define their personal and professional goals. They are creatives who have taken a nontraditional route, refusing to buy into defined stereotypes and social expectations. They have children and run firms and serve their communities and families in ways that are valuable and true, and they don't care if they don't fit the mold. They fit their own molds. They define their own successes.

They don't get there without discomfort. And they certainly didn't get there by asking for permission. They don't stay there without a shield of tough skin and a backbone of support. When we accept other people's uncomfortableness or judgments of our personal leadership, we let it roll off of us. And then we realize that someone else's viewpoint of us is not a reflection of our worth. We grow and come to understand ourselves more than ever before because we see we are free to make the choices for ourselves that make the most sense for us and for those we love.

INTERNAL CHECK:

Who Is Leading You?

It is easy to associate positions and titles with leadership. I would argue that the most important person you lead every day is *you*. We should recognize the courage it takes us women to daily lead *ourselves* and the responsibility we have to the little eyes that may be watching us, the younger generation of women coming up behind us. Here's an exercise to get you thinking:

1) List the first people who come to mind when you think of the word *leader*.

2) List the first people who come to mind when you hear *women leaders*.

3) If someone were to call you a leader, what thoughts come
   to your mind?

4) Do you see yourself as a leader? Why or why not?

5) Are there aspects of your life that you feel you lead? Why
   or why not? In what aspects of your life do you feel you
   follow others?

Just One Yes

Very early in my career, I wanted to pursue a research project. No one
in my department was doing clinical research, as the culture was focused
on other aspects of medicine. To be successful, I needed grant funding
to pay for the research. A requirement for the grant application was that
I needed to publish pilot data. I needed to focus: to understand what it
took to write a grant, to find mentors to help, to learn the ins and outs
of grant writing, and to publish the data. I would have to devote time
and resources for a minimum of a year to this project if I was going to
write a somewhat-competitive grant application. Even doing all of this
while spending a few years assimilating the data, my proposal could still
be rejected.

The odds were definitely against me. Not only was no one in my
department able to mentor me, the National Institute of Health typically granted less than 3 percent of its total grants to anesthesiologists.
It wasn't looking great for me. On top of it all, our department was in a
transition period, and we didn't have a permanent chair of anesthesiology. Our interim chair was a neurosurgeon. He didn't know me, he didn't

understand my research as it wasn't his specialty, and he would be in the position for only a short time. I sought advice from more experienced people in my department, and I didn't hear promising news.

"He isn't going to give you what you need. He isn't going to make sweeping changes when he's an interim chairman," counseled several of my well-meaning colleagues. "It's not on the top of his agenda," they said. "His job is to keep the department afloat, not to develop you," one of my partners said.

Undaunted, I made an appointment to talk to him. He listened as I pleaded my case. I was asking for time—one day a week for a year—to work on my research and apply for a grant. I asked him to bet on me. He did. It turned out to be a good return on his investment.

Over the course of a few years, with little to zero time outside of my clinical duties, I applied for thirteen grants. I was rejected over and over, but with each grant application, I became a little better at writing them. My scores raised until finally I got *one* yes. More than anything, the entire process taught me persistence. I learned how to bounce back from a failure and use it as a springboard toward future success. I also learned to be relentless in the pursuit of something I wanted to create.

"I'VE LEARNED SOMETHING IN EVERY DEAL I'VE negotiated," attorney Aimee Lowe says. "You don't grow in wisdom unless you walk through it. You can exhibit grace and kindness yet still be firm. If you are centered in who you are and in what you require, it makes no difference what anyone else says. You hold the keys to success even in the midst of the storm, resistance, and denial."

Asking Permission to Be Ourselves

As I reflect on how much I learned in that time of struggling to obtain the grant, one truth always strikes me. When my chair agreed to give me the time to pursue my research, my partners took notice. I basically had asked them permission to ask my chair, and they had told me no. It made me so uncomfortable to admit to them that I went against their advice and asked anyway. I realize this sounds crazy, but I stressed so much about telling them I was awarded the very thing they told me not to ask for.

Back then it was a big deal for me to ask for what I wanted, something no one else in my department, especially a woman, had done. I was a junior, clueless in many regards, but I had to believe in myself and go against the current culture. Now I look back and think, *Why on earth would I ask permission to be myself from others who didn't share my goals and objectives?* It seems so silly, but I desperately wanted their approval, and I didn't want to face the social backlash that came with stepping outside the box and being authentic. I wanted to keep my likability factor high. I didn't want to be labeled as "too much." When the chair graciously granted me the time to work on my research and took a chance on me, I was shocked. I spent weeks trying to figure out how I would break it to the people who really had no say in the matter and no control of my life, but I had somehow given them the driver's seat of my professional life. Perhaps you can relate.

As women, we ask for permission from others when really the answer is inside ourselves—it always has been. We ask our colleagues, our partners, and our families for their advice or what we should do. We ask permission from people who have no say in how we are to live because we want to be liked and accepted. We feel this enormous pull to please everyone and explain our choices until the other party can grasp the million excuses we make for why we must be authentic.

The truth is, most of the time, we don't need to ask permission to ask for what we want, and we certainly don't need to ask to live authentically. I look back to that time and imagine God with His head in his hands saying, "Is this going to be your story? Asking permission to ask permission? For the love of Me and all that is holy, just ask!"

Bless me. Sometimes I think God sends me notes in different ways, and like the Tooth Fairy leaving me a quarter under my pillow, I expect to find them. The overarching theme of these notes is something to the effect of: "Dear Sash, I made you. Please be you. Yours Truly, Dad."

It takes strength to be your own boss, to step out and say, "This is the path I am going to take." Those paths come complete with low-hanging branches that snag our shirts, underbrush that trips us once in a while, and difficult terrain that feels unscalable at the moment. It's hard to make mistakes when everyone's watching, especially after you've been granted permission to do what you want. It takes persistence, grit, and grace to be your own boss. But when we are brave enough to step out and ask for that promotion or we announce, "Hey world, I am living this way!" we discover the key to succeeding as our authentic selves.

SUSAN PITT, MD, MPHS, IS AN ENDOCRINE SURGEON AND
Assistant Professor of Surgery at the University of Wisconsin. "When I was in my first fellowship training to become an abdominal organ transplant and hepatopancreatobiliary surgeon, I realized that I was not happy and knew that I needed a change. In surgery, changing your mind was synonymous with failure and weakness, and I felt incredible shame. I was strongly discouraged from going in a different direction and was warned that I might be committing career suicide," Susan explained. "It was as if I was choosing to become a leper or an outcast.

"I changed my specialty, took a year off, got a master's degree in Population Health Science, and went on to do a second fellowship in endocrine surgery at one of the best institutions in the country," Susan said. "While choosing a different path was hard, it led to my landing my dream job.

"Most of the pushback came before I made the switch from transplant to endocrine surgery. Once I made the switch, I was astounded by the number of people who saw my actions as bold, brave, and courageous. I remember one particular vascular surgery fellow saying to me, 'Aren't you going to get bored taking out thyroids and doing the same surgery over and over again?' Despite multiple comebacks that flashed into my mind, I simply replied with grace. 'No. I am sorry that's how you see endocrine surgery. I am going to love it!' And I do," Susan said.

"I would advise other women to ignore the naysayers and all of the voices that warn you can't do something, and believe in the voices that say you can. Through this trial, I learned to believe in myself, face my fears head-on, carry my head high no matter how I am feeling, and most important, to show up for myself," Susan stated.

Okay with No

Through my organization, Brave Enough, I hear from women every day who write and tell me of a problem they have. I meet women from all over the world through conferences and classes I teach. Women often ask for advice or perhaps just a little encouragement. I often don't have any great words of wisdom as the majority of these women are brilliant and more qualified than I am to speak to their situations. But what is interesting about these messages is that a common theme emerges. Most situations can be solved by the woman asking for something. Isn't that the very basic definition of what communication is? An ask?

Sometimes it's asking to receive something they know they have earned: time off, a well-deserved promotion, or a salary increase. Sometimes it's asking for an apology for a wrong done to them. Often times, it's asking their own hearts to forgive themselves and to extend grace to the deepest parts of their hearts, the tiny crevices where the shame seeps out.

Because so much of living authentically requires embracing the necessity of asking for things you need: space, time, salary, freedom, or boundaries. It's what I call *an authenticity essential*. We must be all right with asking, which means we must get comfortable hearing no.

When asking for what we want and need, we will from time to time hear the word *no*. Hearing no often feels like we've asked for the wrong thing. Or that we were wrong to ask in the first place, or that we aren't deserving of whatever we are asking for. We women are hardwired to be advocates for everyone but ourselves. It is often why we hide behind a martyr's mask as we let our own health and well-being slide, and why we celebrate and idolize mothers who do nothing for themselves in the name of doing everything for their children.

But here's the thing: We must be advocates for ourselves, for our authentic selves, especially if we want the next generation of women to be able to ask for the things they deserve and need while not feeling one iota of guilt or shame in doing so. I don't know about you, but I want that for my daughter.

I often hear women say, "I just need to learn to negotiate better." That may be true, but I believe the real truth here is that we must learn to ask more and more and more. We must increase the frequency by being brave enough to ask over and over for what we need. And when we are rejected and told no, we keep asking. You can have great negotiation skills, but if you don't have the courage to ask, and ask again when you are told no, you will have a hard time living as authentically you.

A secret shift happens when you are brave enough to ask for what you need (which oftentimes are boundaries) to live as your authentic self. When you ask, you may be told no at first. But a shift occurs. Suddenly you believe you deserve whatever it is you are asking for, and those whom you are asking know that you mean business. Others take note that you believe in yourself, your cause, and your authenticity. The next time you ask, you will be taken a little more seriously than before. Why? Because others see that you believe in you and that you are worthy. Ah! Do you see this beautiful, wonderful truth?

A Brave Step Forward

Years ago I was speaking with a friend of mine, Laurie, who is equal parts executive and innovator. She's a dreamer and a risk taker. She believes in you more than you believe in yourself. Her audacity is contagious, and ten minutes with Laurie leaves you feeling like you could walk on Wall Street and demand the corner office in the highest building.

I was telling her about a vacant leadership position in my organization and how I was wondering who would be brought in to fill the void. She said, "What about you?" at which point I choked on my LaCroix.

"Me?" I asked, laughing hysterically. "I am an assistant professor! There is no way they would give me that job."

"But could you do it?" Laurie asked.

"Maybe," I replied.

"If you threw your hat into the ring, you'd be declaring something about yourself," Laurie said. "Everyone would take you seriously."

Laurie's words have stuck with me for almost a decade. I didn't apply for the job, for I was much too scared, young, and inexperienced, but her lesson here prompted me to apply for the next job I wanted, which, if not for her words, I would have waited to apply for until I "felt" I was ready. And you know what? People took notice. She was right.

Looking back, I wasn't ready for the job. I was unprepared, but more important, I was unsupported. Taking a stretch job when I did not have appropriate mentors or sponsors could have been detrimental to my career. But I think it is worth noting that if I had been asked to take that job today, years later, I still would feel unprepared. The difference is that I would have mentors and sponsors to support me, and thus I would feel braver and more courageous to take the risk and know I wouldn't fail.

But more significant, I saw the value in asking myself to step forward. I understood that I didn't need to have everything 100 percent figured out to advocate for what I wanted and needed. When I compared myself with my competition, I realized that the men were great at asking for things, oftentimes well before they "deserved" them. While I patiently waited for someone to recognize my worth and offer to me the things I wanted, the men were stepping forward, asking, often being rejected, and then asking again.

Where was I? Likely having to tell myself not to be upset because I didn't get the position while trying to improve what I perceived to be gaps so I could ask again. We cannot be afraid to be bossy, to be authentic, to be gritty, and to bestow grace. We are made to be women for a reason—and I would like to think that the most important thing we women can do is to step into our own style of leadership, beginning with leading ourselves.

Wouldn't it be a lovely day if we could go to work, engage in our communities, and do so without wasting brain space on whether we were too much of this or too little of that? Wouldn't it be life altering if we had the courage to ask for the things we need and deserve, unafraid or unabashed to hear the word *no*? Wouldn't it be great to let criticism we receive and backlash we experience roll off us as though we were untouched?

There is a way to do this, and it starts with us. Then it involves each other. Yup. When we allow other women to be authentic, we then feel more comfortable and courageous to live out our authenticity. Have I lost you? Be bossy. It's okay. Then, look around and see who else is being bossy.

She's your people. You need her. You'll see.

CHECKING IN WITH YOURSELF *Exercise 6*

Grab your journal and let's go inward to think about how we succeeded as girls. The way we were taught to succeed as girls may be limiting our success as women.

1) Think back to when you were a child. Were you rewarded for speaking up or taking charge, or were you rewarded for being compliant?

_____

_____

_____

2) Have you ever been called bossy? Have you ever apologized for being bossy? What were the circumstances?

_____

_____

_____

3) Think about something you would like to do—maybe launch a new project or get a promotion or step into a new position. Are you waiting for someone to give you permission, to pick you, or to call on you?

_____

_____

_____

Chapter 7

Finding Your Five

Good friends help you to find important
things when you have lost them...your smile,
your hope, and your courage.

—*Doe Zantamata, American author* [1]

The Power of a Woman Tribe

s I drove home from the hospital one evening after a heart-wrenching day, it hit me. I had thirty minutes left in my commute to process what had happened. Once home I would step into my other role of mom, and put aside my role as a doctor. Thirty minutes to think through the grief I had experienced that day. Although sadness permeated me, I also thought about the need for a new dress for an upcoming event. What kind of dress would be appropriate to wear to this event? I needed some input, some advice. Suddenly, I wished I could call a friend. A girlfriend. Where had mine gone?

After having four kids in seven years while finishing medical school, residency and training, and then starting my career as an attending anesthesiologist, I had let my friendships slip. It was as if I couldn't hold on to so many things, and so I had dropped those that felt unnecessary and selfish. My health was number one, and my relationships with other women was a close second. Life had been moving so fast, I hadn't really noticed. Now I was lonely, and it was no one's fault but my own.

On that drive home, passing row after row of cornfields, I realized how much I missed having girlfriends. I missed laughing hysterically with them over the realities of our lives. I missed celebrating wins and losses together. I missed talking to them. Sharing life with them.

I remembered reflecting once with a work colleague about how much fun college was, mainly because of the close friendships I had developed. She agreed with me, and when I said I wish I had those friends at this time of my life, she said something quite honest and provoking: "We don't get to have friendships at this stage. We are raising our families and starting careers. It's not the time for it."

Her statement resonated with me, but it also didn't feel right. It was like she was justifying my loneliness, and probably her own. It was as if she was telling me, "Please don't add one more thing to my plate that makes me feel guilty. Now is not the time for fun and games."

While I agreed I had little free time to even shower daily during those years, let alone meet a friend for a cup of coffee, I disagreed with the premise that to have friends was selfish and shouldn't be encouraged. I rebelled against the notion that nurturing friendships and finding joy in others when starting your career and raising a family is unjustified. Isn't the time when we are *most* vulnerable to feeling unworthy, to isolation, to burnout and losing our sense of identity, to battling anxiety and depression, and feeling inadequate on a daily basis (otherwise known as our thirties) when we need supportive peer relationships the greatest?

After that lonely drive home during my year in the desert, I came to myself. I was slowly discovering that I had been empty and broken for quite some time. I realized that in my struggle, I was hiding from my friends, my family, and myself. When you're hiding, the last thing you want anyone to see is the real you. I had definitely been hiding.

As you emerge from your cave of insecurity and inadequacy, your hiding place, when you become a little braver each day to face life as the authentic you, you realize that you need support so you don't slip back into hiding again.

INTERNAL CHECK:

Reconnecting with Dear Friends

It is easy to lose our friendships as we enter incredibly busy periods of our lives. New jobs, relocations, and raising families can easily distract us from maintaining friendships. Reconnecting with past friends or establishing new friends does not have to be overwhelming. The following are some steps that helped me reengage with women friends:

1) Make a list of one to three women you enjoy being around.

2) Call them (I prefer this over email or text) and tell them that you recognize it's been a long time since you've had any contact. Say that you need a friend and really want to reconnect.

3) Be honest with them and share one or two wins in your life and one or two struggles. You will be amazed at how much these shares can work to reconnect you!

4) Make a commitment (put a reminder in your phone) to reach out weekly. Text, email, or call, even if it's a quick voice mail! Share one win and one loss or struggle.

When I made the effort to nurture my lapsed friendships, it unleashed something unexpected and powerful. As well as finding comfort and camaraderie, I found inspiration. I found truth. When we take the time to develop healthy friendships, we find critical truths that become water in times of drought. These affirmations, told to us through the actions of our friends, include the following:

- It is perfectly normal to fail.
- You are allowed to work on yourself.
- You are allowed to have fun with friends.
- It is vital to put your own health first.
- There is not one but likely *several* women who are struggling with your exact demons.
- True friends give you a valuable reflection of yourself.
- It's all right to experience negative feelings and emotions.
- Nearly every trial you have experienced has been overcome by a woman similar to you.

Strong female friendships with women who accept you, root for you, and forgive you show you that you *can* be your authentic self and still be loved. This is beyond empowering. It is most necessary at the stage in your life when you feel you don't have time for it.

Let's face it: cultivating friendships at a point when your job and family commitments leave you with little time to even brush your teeth presents a challenge. But oftentimes having one or two close friends, whether connected to your work life or completely separate, may be your lifeline.

As women we are so used to surviving and hiding, we don't know any other way to live. We feel guilty when we add nurturing aspects of our lives, such as friendships with other women, in an effort to thrive. We don't know how to accept friendships or all of the lovely facets that come with them. At first it may feel like being handed a Chanel bag at a soccer game as it's starting to rain. *What the heck am I supposed to do with this?*

Friendships during our busiest years, when we are launching careers and raising little ones whom we find in our beds at 3:00 AM asking for pancakes, feel inappropriate. It's as if friendships are an extravagance of joy that we have no right to claim at this busy intersection.

What did you say? Joy? How dare you! If we ourselves don't believe we deserve joy at this stage of life, then we likely don't believe we deserve friends. But we need dear friends to remind us of the part of us that is not mother, doctor, lawyer, teacher, chef, daughter, or wife. We need friends to remind us that we can still develop our unique traits, dreams, and passions. That they have a place in this world and in our lives. That we can experience joy in the midst of trials, build memories even when we aren't at our goal weight, and believe we are more than the sum of our worst days.

Close girlfriends can do that for us. They can throw a lifeline into the pit we find ourselves in (or were pushed into) and pull us out. Or they can send us down a glass of pinot or a double shot latte with whip if we'd like to stay and ponder a while.

> *"My mind is a neighborhood*
> *I try not to go into alone."*
>
> —Anne Lamott, American author

Female Friendships: Not Optional

Friendships can also feel like a chore, like going to the gym. One more thing we have to accomplish in our day, one more thing to feel guilty about because we didn't achieve. That's not the point of this chapter. The last thing I want is to make you feel more guilt. Women supporting women is not a given, particularly in the workplace. If we distrust our female colleagues, compete with them, and obstruct their professional advancement, we also hurt ourselves.

There is a large body of research on the mental and physical health benefits of having strong social ties. The largest meta-analysis (meta-analysis is a study that looks at all the known research on a specific topic and draws conclusions and summaries) to date shows that along every stage of life, regardless of age, sex, baseline health, or cause of death, having a social support system is directly linked to living a long, healthy life. It is just as protective as not smoking and having low cholesterol.[2] In other words, it is just as important to have friends as it is to eat healthy, exercise, and avoid smoking.

And that's not all. Several studies show that if you are sick or going through a high-stress period in your life, you're much more likely to overcome that situation if you have girlfriends. One of the most interesting areas of the study looked at women with breast cancer. Those who have friends, more than those who have family support, are more likely to survive than women without close friendships.[3] Even more important is that the women who had those friendships at the time of diagnosis had the best odds of a good outcome. In other words, cultivate those friendships now, before life brings you challenges, illnesses, and stress.

Women who have close friends enjoy longer and healthier lives. We need friends to live. When the world makes you feel guilty for spending time with your friends, push back. Doctor's orders.

> *"As you grow older,*
> *you will discover*
> *that you have two hands,*
> *one for helping yourself,*
> *the other for helping others."*
>
> —Audrey Hepburn

During my year in the desert, I discovered how very lonely and isolated I was. How had this happened? I always considered myself a friendly person, a caring person. But that was the exact problem.

I was caring for everyone but me. I didn't realize that part of caring for myself required having friends. I hadn't linked the two facts: self-care and friendships with other women. I thought spending time cultivating friendships was selfish. I didn't understand how badly I needed social support to really be the best, healthiest me—for my patients, for my family, and for myself. In my attempt to take care of everyone, I had let this critical piece of my mental well-being slide. I had isolated myself and told myself that the lack of friendships was just part of this stage of my life.

You may be reading this and thinking that this is where you are. You may feel isolated or lonely, as if you are stranded on a deserted island. You may not know even where to begin to find a friend. Can you pick up one at Trader Joe's? Order one on Amazon?

It can feel overwhelming and scary to open yourself to friendship. You know why? You have to be vulnerable. You have to be real. You have to show up to friendship and say, "Hey. This is me. I don't remember the last time I washed my hair, and I just spent $200 on anti-aging products and dark chocolate almonds at Target. How are you?"

I know this feeling, sister, because I have been there. When I realized how lonely I felt and how much I needed friends, I did something out of the norm for me. I sent out a bat signal and asked others to be my friend. I am not saying you should adopt my methodology for finding a tribe, but I learned the importance of establishing female friendships and want to share it with you.

I needed women with whom I could relate. I also needed friendships that would be encouraging, empowering, and real. Honestly, I didn't know where to find them. So I sent out a text to a small group of women whom I knew from different aspects of life—around my age, similar jobs, some with kids and some without—and asked them to join a text group. I basically said, "Hey, do you want to be my friend?"

I started texting positive encouragement to my group, and they responded with inspiring and supportive texts. We shared funny stories and life experiences and day-to-day challenges. We shared makeup tips and work wins and, well, we shared *life*.

Having this small group of friends in my phone when I needed them filled a void in my life. I laughed more, felt more confident with my decisions, and experienced a sense of strength that allowed me to bounce back from mishaps. Mostly, I felt my struggles and self-doubts were normal. I realized my ideas and thoughts belonged—I belonged, just as I was. Having friendships with like-minded women was like receiving a daily dose of courage. I felt brave. I felt *brave enough*.

From this text group, I contemplated an idea. What if there was a place online for more women to find one another? What if other women needed encouragement to keep striving, who needed to hear their ideas were valued, their challenges were normal, and they mattered? I wondered if other women were out there, just like me, needing a daily dose of courage to get through their days *as a woman*. I wondered if they, too, needed to be brave enough.

IN 2015 I CONTACTED A HANDFUL OF WOMEN I KNEW WHO shared my profession and similar struggles as mine. While this group grew into what is now called Style MD, a group of over ten thousand practicing women physicians, these women became my daily lifeline. Developing a tribe is not outside the reach of any woman and is significantly powerful. Think of a few women who may live apart, work in different arenas, but may be at similar life stages. I encourage you to reach out to these women via email or text and form a group. You will be surprised at how a group of women can empower, encourage, and uplift one another and share wisdom, life knowledge, and thus power.

Power in the Collective

I started an online community of women physicians. As I scrolled through a list of my contacts, I thought, *Should I add her to the group? Will she think I am crazy?* I added thirty women physicians I knew from across the country to the group. I posted on many different topics, from encouragement for women facing bias to practical advice—like what to wear to a job interview. I wanted women physicians to have a safe place to ask the questions they would ask a friend and not feel like they were at risk of being judged.

I had hoped to grow a small community whose members would support one another. I could not have predicted how the group would flourish into a tribe ten thousand women strong or what the women in the group would teach me. The group, Style MD, became a spectacular group of women who taught me many important life truths. They taught me that friendship is *power*.

The women in Style MD made me realize there was more to my identity than being a wife, a doctor, and a mom. The group revealed to me that when women see the best in others, they can change one another's confidence and internal mind-set. When women have a supportive tribe, they become the best version of themselves.

You may be thinking, *Now she's telling me I need friends? Great. Add it to the list. Just one more thing I need to do. One more thing I need to add to my life.* Hold on. Or maybe you are thinking of a time when a friend deeply hurt you, and you don't want to risk heartbreak again. I know what it is like to lose a close friendship. It is not an easy bump in the road. It hurts and can make you doubt yourself and your perception of people. You may have built impenetrable walls around your heart and mind to protect yourself from further betrayal.

I am here to tell you that friendships with women can be messy. Like anything valuable, female friendships can test you, especially when the parties come from different backgrounds and see the world differently. I often hear from women how previous female relationships have hurt them, and they don't think establishing a new friendship is worth the time or effort. They tell me about competing with other women, which is often the result of our society restricting opportunities for women and creating an illusion that there is a limited amount of success for women.

True friendships are like any relationship. They take trust, vulnerability, honesty, and resilience. They require you to work through disagreements, hurt feelings, jealous thoughts and actions, and misunderstandings. We often tell ourselves that if we had the perfect friend, she would never compete with us, be jealous of us, hurt our feelings, or lose touch. But that is simply not the case. We ourselves are not perfect, and thus we should not expect our friendships to be. Whether it's a coworker who has become a friend or someone we met through Facebook, female friendships require work. We must extend grace to even our closest friends and not give up on relationships with other women. We must be gritty—fight for our friendships—and extend grace—forgive.

Relationships with other women are worth every bump in the road. When you are brave enough to develop alliances with other women, you can see yourself through another person's eyes. A person who has your back, sees you at your worst, and loves you anyway. She straightens your crown when it's crooked. She takes your sword and brandishes it for you when you are tired of fighting and need rest. It is amazing what you can create when you reach out to other women and see the best in them.

CASEY LEWIS, MD, IS A PEDIATRICIAN WHO FOUNDED HER own clinics, Pediatrics of Bullitt County, in Kentucky. Casey built an alliance with a girlfriend, also a pediatrician right out of training, and together they went into business. She also serves on the Board of Directors of MagMutual, one of the largest medical professional liability insurance companies in the country.

"During a time when nearly all new graduates became hospital employees or joined existing practices, I decided to start my own private pediatric practice. Along with my best friend and fellow lady-boss, Sarah Hart, MD, we built a practice from the ground up. We used our homes as collateral for our business loan and dove in headfirst. Within five years, we had two locations and over eight thousand patients. Ten years later, we continue to grow. We now have eight providers and own the buildings our practices are in," Casey stated.

"At my residency graduation, my program director announced each graduate's planned path. As I walked across the stage, with my colleagues and family in the audience, he said 'Casey is going to start her own practice,' then sarcastically added, 'Good luck with that.' I smiled my biggest smile and kept on walking. I think I've proved to him that luck wasn't needed," Casey said. "Being underestimated is my superpower, and I tell other women to embrace it. My Southern upbringing taught me that a big smile can be your best negotiating tool.

"I naïvely never considered that starting my practice would be anything other than a success. Some may say that our practice is very successful because of our balance sheet or because we consistently recruit the top graduates in each residency class. I define it as successful because we practice excellent medicine and treat our patients with kindness and respect," Casey explained.

The Vulnerability of Friends

At times I have completely withdrawn from friendships. I told myself I had nothing to give others, so I stopped connecting. I hid from my friends because, in truth, I was hiding from myself. I didn't want to be the friend with issues that brought the group down, or I didn't want to share the insecurities, failures, or problems I was going through. I convinced myself that my friends would like me only when I was sunshine, rainbows, and rosé.

Here's my story, my truth: I haven't always had a throng of friends, and I haven't always been the best friend I could be. I am sharing the hard stuff with you because you are taking the time to read this book and hearing what I've learned along the journey. There have been times when I convinced myself I was too busy for friends, not "well enough" for friends, or not "fun enough" for friends. Basically, I believed I was not enough.

Until you realize that where you are right now is a worthy place, until you see your value as a human as enough just as you are, and you are worth surrounding yourself with others, you will not grow. You will not be the friend your friends and your future friends need until you realize *you are enough*.

Dr. Brené Brown, who has studied vulnerability for more than a decade and published her research on the subject, has demonstrated that vulnerability is central to strong social connections.[4] Basically, if we want genuine friendships, which are just as important to our health as exercise and diet, we must be real with those friends. We must show our scars and insecurities and share our failures.

Friendships with women who know when your clothes don't fit, when your marriage isn't perfect, and when you're struggling at work are *authentic*. And they hold power for you because they are based on an *authentic you*. Not the all-Spanx, all-smiles, all-glitter yet empty version of you; the real you. The messy, imperfect one.

Do you see why friendships with women are worth disagreements, hard moments of misunderstandings, and apologies to one another when we miss the mark? They force us to accept ourselves as the most authentic version of ourselves—the person we are *now*. They make us reveal who we really are, all the good and the bad, and lead us to recognize we are our best when we are real. They are life-giving, confidence building, and a powerful mechanism of personal change.

Perhaps you are reading this and thinking of five hundred reasons why you can't invest in female friendships. You are too busy. You are too broken. You are too introverted. You don't know where to find a friend, or you've tried in the past and failed. I want to bust the five most common myths I hear from women on why they can't have friends. Why they're unique, and why friendships with other women just aren't possible. In my coaching classes, and in talking to hundreds of women from all over the world at events and retreats, these five myths are on continuous repeat. I want to address them and empower you.

Busting the Friendship Myths

Deep breath, sister. Open your mind. Rosé or latte in hand. Ready? News flash: you aren't special. Don't take this the wrong way, but there's nothing in your life that is "too" anything for a friend. Nope. You don't get a free pass here. You're not busier than the rest of us, more messed up, or some level of scared the rest of us don't understand. Sorry, Charlie's angel. You need friends. You need friends as much as you need oxygen.

Friendship Myth #1: I am too busy for friends.

Reality: You are too busy.

If you do not have one hour a month to meet a friend, then you are too busy. You likely need to reset your boundaries and dive deep into your priorities. Oftentimes I meet a friend for breakfast, coffee, or a walk early Saturday mornings. I call these power moments. As a busy mother of four with a full-time job, I can't get away most nights. But early Saturday I can escape for a power hour with a friend who I know will be there for me when the times get rough.

Friendship Myth #2: I don't have opportunities to meet friends.

Reality: Unless you live like the Unabomber, friend potentials are everywhere. Yes, everywhere.

Do you go to work? To the gym? To church? Do you belong to any groups on social media? You can find a friend. Wherever there are women, there are friend potentials. What it requires is openness and a bit of courage. I have reached out to women and asked them, "Will you be my friend?" You may be laughing, but it is true. I have discovered that most women feel similarly: they need friendships, they often struggle to find them, and most are open to forging new ones.

We often think that women would never be interested in forming an alliance with us. We form preconceived judgments, based on our biases and past experiences, regarding how other women must think about us. But the truth is, there are women out there who are similar to us. They may not look like us, talk like us, or do the same work we do, but I guarantee you they have similar struggles.

Do you know what research has demonstrated to produce deep bonds and strong relationships? A shared struggle or a shared mission. A good example is veterans who served together through conflicts. They possess tight bonds and deep connections.[5] Similarly, studies have demonstrated that communities who experience natural disasters and turmoil find themselves with stronger social connections after the event.

I would argue that during our most strenuous times of life, when we may feel we aren't our best and are dropping balls right and left, we have the capacity to form the strongest relationships with other women who are likely experiencing similar challenges. Life itself, as a woman who is trying to live by the *man*-ual, represents a shared struggle. We just need a little courage to look to our right and left and say, "Hey, want to be my friend?"

Friendship Myth #3: I am not outgoing, so I can't make friends.

Reality: You don't have to change your personality to make friends.

I am an extroverted person, but the most interesting thing is that my closest friends are all introverts. I am also married to an introvert. Most of us at some point experience social anxiety, regardless of where we are on the introvert-extrovert spectrum. We are scared to approach someone, afraid to put ourselves out there and face possible rejection, or fear being vulnerable. Those are universal experiences independent of most people's personalities (unless you are a narcissist, and in that case, bless you).

I understand that fear of rejection is a sliding scale, different for each of us concerning our various challenges and strengths. But the truth is, if we were all social butterflies, we wouldn't have near the depth of relationships and diversity of understanding we do! We need one another. We need quiet friends, loud friends, funny friends, and serious friends. We need friends who listen, friends who make us laugh until we cry, and friends who hold our hands in the darkest of times.

If they haven't already darkened your life, rough times will come. What if you, just as you are, are holding the life vest another sister needs? Be brave. Reach out.

Friendship Myth #4: Women are mean. It's easier to be friends with guys and avoid women altogether.

Reality: For every woman who has knocked you down, ten are willing to pull you up.

I hear the "women are mean" myth so much I had to include it. To be honest, I didn't want to give it any space in this book, but it is one of the most important limiting beliefs we must unlearn if we women are to advance. This common excuse I hear for why women don't pursue female friendships makes me incredibly sad.

As I previously described in Chapter 3, many women distance themselves from feminine traits in the workplace and try to achieve success in the manner a man would. The social construct that is designed to limit women in power positions perpetuates the very thing we are fighting against: women must compete against other women to get ahead. The fact that we have been a minority group fighting for scarce resources can often promote interpersonal stiff-arms, closed doors, and competitiveness.

No, no, and a big fat no! I reject this, and I am asking you to do the same. No study has shown, or even been done, that women hold back more women than men do. It is unfounded. The scarcity mentality of "only a few women can be in power" creates a limited opportunity construct. The scant number of women holding positions at the top has perpetuated the mistaken thought that women are meaner to one another than men are to other men. What has been shown is that *both* women and men have biases toward women. True. But the myth that women are "meaner" is likely another way for society to limit us through fear, having us believe that when our lights shine bright, it dims the lights of the women around us and causes mass hysteria and girl fights.

Do women hurt other women? Sometimes. All of us have likely been hurt by a woman or two. Do women hold women back more than men? No. Do communities and cultures in which women help other women advance women? Yes. One study done regarding women at West Point showed exactly that: when women support one another, great things happen.[6] The researchers studied the gender peer effects of a random group of West Point Military Academy cadets. They compared how different groups of men and women cadets scored and progressed through the rigorous training and performance tests over their years in the academy. They found that "women do significantly better when placed in companies with more women peers. The addition of one woman peer reduced the gender progression gap by half," according to the study's findings.

Maybe we think women are more hateful toward us because we expect more from them. As Madeline Albright said: "There's a special place in hell for women who don't help each other."[7] I've often thought of how bias plays into this. Are we harder on women, more judgmental in the way they treat us, because we expect more from them? Is it another burden we carry as women that we must be even kinder to other women than are our male colleagues, and when we are not, we are judged more harshly?

The fact is, it is probable that a woman has hurt your feelings, possibly creating distrust in female friendships. It is even more possible that a woman will offend you or disappoint you in the future. After all, this is life. In my experience, my view of people is directly dependent on my current view of myself. When I am living authentically and demonstrating self-compassion to myself, I am more likely to extend that to the people I do life with—many of whom are women.

For about ten years I served on several national committees on which only one or two other members were women. One was quite the opposite of me in many ways, yet we shared a similar area of study, and I admired her work ethic and ideas. For as much as I leaned one way, she leaned the other. I tried to be friendly, but it was obvious she wasn't a Sasha fan. She appeared to contradict me at every turn, and then I started making judgments about her.

She doesn't like me, I would think. Though she never told me she wasn't on Team Sasha, I created a narrative that said so. The story in my head was that because she was different from me, and because she wasn't as outgoing as me and didn't smile at me when I looked at her, she didn't like me. I was convinced she thought I wasn't as bright as her, as competent as her, and that she was judging me and my non–Ivy League education.

For nearly ten years when we ran into each other, even when we were the only two women in the room, we avoided each other…until one day, something unpredictable happened.

A mutual colleague said to me while in her company, "Sasha, you have a blog?" I cringed. I didn't want my frenemy to know about my blog. It would just be one more example of how I wasn't as serious an academician as her (you see, the story I had created in my head about this woman said that she was judging me and didn't think I was as smart as her). Internally dying, ashamed of my authentic self, and being vulnerable in front of this woman, I slowly answered and explained my blog.

Three hours later I was in my hotel room after the meeting. I received a text message from this woman. She asked if we could meet in the hotel lobby before our evening event. My heart raced with instant anxiety. *Is she going to shame me? Rip me a new one? Make fun of me?* These thoughts and more swirled in my head.

I met this woman in the lobby. I was stunned when she complimented me on my blog! She said she admired me and identified with my writing. She shared that she, too, struggled with many of the things I had written about. She then asked me something that drastically changed our story: "Sasha, why don't you like me?"

Since then, I have learned so much from this woman. You see, my manufactured thoughts had fed a story in which she didn't like me and thought I was not as smart as her (which is likely true since she is brilliant!). My beliefs, which held no merit, created a distance between us. I then enacted the stereotype I was convinced of: she was a mean girl, and she didn't like me. The result had put us both in defensive mode.

Now this woman and I are allies. We support each other at meetings and chuckle at the years we wasted on opposite sides of the table as we worked to avoid each other. We found that while we are very different in many ways, we are alike in the ways that matter. We are both physicians, both committed to helping the next generation of women, and both able to see where we need to improve. We encourage, sponsor, and cheer for each other.

Give the women around you a chance. Give them the same grace you give yourself. You just might be surprised to find the ally you didn't know you needed.

Friendship Myth #5: If I show my friends who I really am, they won't stick around.

Truth: True friends love you more for your imperfections than they ever will for your accomplishments.

Think about this: What do you love about the people you do life with? Do you love them because they display perfect lives, are perfect sizes, have perfect jobs, and enjoy perfect postcard-worthy families? No. The people we love most in the world are those who are honest with us. They are not afraid to show their scars and warts. They make us feel comfortable in our own imperfect skin, and they accept us for who we are.

It is the same with friendships. Our strongest social connections are rooted in the fact that we are not perfect and make mistakes, and yet we trust one another to remain with us through the storms. Sharing our imperfections creates strong bonds and should encourage us to seek friendships with other women. If a friend leaves us when life gets hard, well, we are probably better off on the journey without that person.

A small group of close friends (whom I refer to as "my five"), versus a long list of superficial friendships, provides anti-aging benefits. Research on over three hundred thousand people showed that having strong social connections can influence the length of a person's life just as much as being a nonsmoker. In other words, friendships with other women can be both protective and helpful in times of stress.[8] Friendship is power.

My five are my lifeline. They are the ones I text in tears from my closet when I feel like I'm failing as a parent and want to escape motherhood and all it entails. They are the ones I call when I receive a harsh review or critique that threatens to send me spiraling into self-doubt. They are the ones I contact when I've achieved the speaking gig I've been working for years to land or when my son scores the winning goal. They are my cheering squad and my sounding board.

Too often we don't prioritize having friends because we are busy building careers and raising families. We even feel guilty when we spend time with friends, thinking of it as frivolous. My hope is that this chapter has convinced you that far from being impractical, finding "your five" is essential.

When was the last time you allowed yourself to have fun with friends? When was the last time you had a power hour with a friend and left better for it? Perhaps it's time to give yourself permission.

CHECKING IN WITH YOURSELF   *Exercise 7*

Grab your journal and complete this exercise on the status of your friendships with other women. Be honest with yourself.

1) Think about your close friendships. List the women you could lean on in times of stress and who embrace you for your authentic self.

   _____

   _____

   _____

2) When was the last time you invested in those friendships?

   _____

   _____

   _____

3) Make a plan to reach out to a friend. Write it down. Tell her how much you appreciate her. Schedule a time to meet for a walk, coffee, lunch—whatever works. Make sure she knows that you value her friendship, and why.

   _____

   _____

   _____

Chapter 8

An Imposter Among Us

The best protection any woman
can have is courage.

—*Elizabeth Cady Stanton,
American abolitionist*[1]

Silencing Your Internal Frenemy

hen I was a junior attending physician and had been in practice for less than two years, I was invited to speak at a large conference on a panel with two other cardiac anesthesiologists. Well-known, they were distinguished senior physicians from Ivy League schools. I had heard them speak multiple times—from a chair in the audience.

My first reaction to the invitation was to email the conference planners and tell them they had made a mistake. There was no way they wanted me to speak. I was a junior expert. Just starting out. I had spoken only one other time on the big stage, and it was a ten-minute presentation. And I wasn't from Harvard; I was from Nebraska.

Has someone ever asked you to do something big, something important, and it caught you by surprise? Your first reaction is "*Me?*" "You want *me* to speak at that conference?" "You want *me* to lead the committee?" "You want *me* to direct this initiative?"

You sit there thinking, *Why is this person asking me? How could they possibly think I could do this task? How could they think I am good enough to do this? Is this a trick?*

Your brain takes an inventory of your previous failures and all the reasons you aren't the woman for the job. All the things you lack and the times you've messed up. Fear envelops you.

What you *don't* think of are all your successes. What doesn't cross your mind is the fact that you were likely asked to fill this job because you have demonstrated skills and expertise, which makes you qualified. So, you say: "No, thank you." Fear wins, and the opportunity goes to someone else.

What you've just experienced is called imposter syndrome. It's a real thing.

Imposter syndrome, or what some call imposter phenomenon, is a serious experience. It's like a chain tied to your ankle, keeping you tethered to a small circle of space. It holds you back. And when someone offers you an opportunity to break free from the chain, you glance down at your ankle and convince yourself you are more comfortable (and safe?) staying put.

Imposter syndrome is defined as the inability to internalize one's accomplishments. It was first described in the 1970s and was found to be associated with high-achieving women.[2] Since that time, it has been studied and published in hundreds of research articles and found that both high-achieving men and women experience it. It is mostly associated with people who possess above-average abilities. If you don't have some measure of imposter syndrome, according to some studies you are more likely to be a low-ability person, have mental illness, or are a narcissist. In other words, if you do experience imposter syndrome, you are in good company. It means you are an achiever and have higher than normal abilities.

The mind-set that overcomes us when we experience imposter syndrome convinces us that our success is fraudulent. Somehow we have faked our way to achievement and tricked people into believing we are smarter, more experienced, and more talented than we are. It is important to recognize when you are experiencing it because research has found that those who routinely experience it are less likely to be promoted, to seek career advances, or report higher job satisfaction.[3,4]

Women struggle with imposter syndrome to a different degree than do men, which is why women wait until they are overqualified for a job before applying, while men tend to try for a promotion or a job change when they meet some, but not all, of the requirements. Research has found that men are more likely to be hired on their *potential*, while women are more apt to be offered a job based on their *likability*.

While both women and men may experience imposter syndrome, there are some differences in what it does to women and men, and most important, how it affects the next thing we do. Some research has demonstrated that men experience high levels of stress and anxiety with imposter syndrome. When men were given negative feedback on a task, they experienced higher levels of stress and anxiety when compared with women. It is thought this is because men have more societal pressure not to fail, as they are expected to achieve. Thus, when men believe their success is fraudulent, they have a higher chance of experiencing anxiety.

On the other hand, when women with imposter syndrome were presented with the same scenario in controlled studies, they had a different reaction to negative feedback such as being told they failed or they didn't measure up. How did the women respond? They tried harder. Why? Because the women were more likely to believe the negative feedback from their bosses and supervisors *as true. As expected.*

We women probably won't experience anxiety when we are told we failed because we tend to believe we are failures. Wow. Is this because we are prone to face obstruction to achieve, or, as my friend Dr. Julie Silver says, we are constantly trying to break through a closed gate, one that should be open for us based on our accomplishments and expertise?

When we have the skills and abilities to do the job but aren't selected, it is a strong signal for us to doubt ourselves. It feeds our imposter syndrome. It makes us believe that our accomplishments are fraudulent, and the gig is up.

So we try harder. We do more. We earn more achievements, attain more degrees, write more papers, appear in more publications, serve on more committees. More, more, and more. And then…we burn out. Or we fail to get the next promotion or achievement, and the cycle continues.

> "Every time I was called on in class, I was sure that I was about to embarrass myself. Every time I took a test, I was sure that it had gone badly. And every time I didn't embarrass myself—or even [when I] excelled—I believed that I had fooled everyone yet again. One day soon, the jig would be up…This phenomenon of capable people being plagued by self-doubt has a name—Impostor Syndrome. Both men and women are susceptible to Impostor Syndrome, but women tend to experience it more intensely and be more limited by it."
>
> —Sheryl Sandberg, *Lean In*

I want you to stop for a moment. Hit pause. Go inward and think of your internal voice. Let's do a check.

What does your internal voice say to you when you receive a compliment? "Thank you! Yes! I am so grateful for my expertise!"? Or "I am a joke. I am fooling everyone"?

What does your internal voice say when someone asks you to do something big, something new, something that requires leadership? Does it say, "HECK, YES! I am so excited about this amazing opportunity!"? Or "Um, what? Me? You've got the wrong woman"?

Or imagine this: Your colleague wants to nominate you for something. You instantly reject this offer and cringe at the thought of stepping up. *No way, not me,* you think. *There's absolutely no way I could. It's just not me.*

I want to challenge you. I want you to think about reframing your thoughts. I want you to look inside yourself and what your internal frenemy is saying to you, and change that internal voice into your internal fangirl.

To do this, we must go through a series of steps. Once we do them, we are far more well informed and able to quickly identify the frenemy voices that speak untruths to us and turn them off. Literally, turn them off.

People often say to me, "I just need more confidence, and then I could do XYZ." The truth is, confidence comes from taking action, from doing what we may be scared to do or what we may not know how to do. Confidence does not come by doing only the things we feel 100 percent ready to do. If you never experience imposter syndrome, you are not giving yourself opportunities to grow your confidence. Remember, confidence is a muscle. You grow it only by stretching it, challenging it, and making it lift heavy things.

Steps to Overcoming the Imposter

The following steps will help you flex your confidence muscles by reframing the thoughts that too often stop you from doing the next, scary, cool thing. The next time you contemplate saying yes to something you've been asked to do or desperately want to do but find yourself doubting your abilities, I encourage you to go through these steps that have helped me.

Step 1. Bravely face the fear. For example, write "I fear I will lose my words and freeze onstage." Where is this coming from? A past failure? Past words spoken by someone? Do you have any evidence that this will happen again or at all? Writing down your fear allows you to objectively view it for what it is: just a thought. Literally.

Step 2. Talk to yourself about the truth of this fear as you would speak to your best friend. What would your friend tell you to do? What would she/he say about this fear? Talk to yourself in the same manner. Tell yourself the truth—what may be difficult in this challenge and what you've done in the past to succeed in similar challenges.

Step 3. Imagine the worst possible scenario. Yep, I want you to go there. Say, for example, your biggest fear is falling off a stage (this has happened to me!). What is the *worst* result of this unlikely event? Process it in your mind. Walk through the uncomfortable scenarios. You will probably discover that the consequences are pretty benign.

Whenever I go through this step, I instantly realize how much I am overexaggerating my fear. I am giving my fear power that I should be giving to my internal fangirl. The truth is, when I walk through the worst fear (for example, I am going to write a book and no one is going to read it, or, they will read it and give me bad reviews), I come to see that I can survive the worst-case scenario. The *outcome* of our fears is often what we dread the most, but they are most times unrealistic, benign, or temporary.

Let's do the worst-case scenario exercise. Mine typically goes something like this: I am asked to speak at a conference with a few thousand attendees. I get up onstage and my slides fail to work. I am standing on stage, staring at the crowd, desperately trying to remember the order of my slides so I can deliver my talk. I fumble through it, relying on my memory, but I fail to deliver, big-time. After the talk, I check social media. Several conference-goers post that they were bummed after hearing me speak. I didn't meet their expectations.

Clearly, if this happened, I would be devastated. But could I have controlled the outcome and made it better? Probably not. I could not control an audiovisual fail. It was outside my hand. Can I guarantee that I will deliver amazing talks every time I stand on a stage? Nope. No way. I am human. What could I do? I can bounce back. I can own the snafu and say, "Yes, my delivery wasn't the best because of human error. Let's move on with grit and with grace." I have conquered a potential fear by running through the worst case in my mind, knowing I would survive.

Step 4. List all the reasons why you were asked to do this task, or why you want to step up to the challenge. Your answer is probably based on your past experiences and successes. List this evidence, and read it next to your fear list. Which one has *more* truth? Which one has more objective evidence?

Now, go slay your fear! Step forward, even if you are scared. You will be amazed at how much more settled you are when you objectively identify the truth of your fear and recognize imposter phenomenon. It is amazing what happens when you decide it is perfectly acceptable to be afraid and do whatever scares you anyway. It is freeing when you have already walked through all the worst-case scenarios in your mind and see the reality of how you would survive it.

> *"Courage is fear that has said its prayers."*
>
> —Dorothy Bernard

Not Quite Enough

I often think about the missed opportunities women have experienced. So often we let our imposter phenomenon and frenemy voices overtake us. Especially when we are young, we often say, "No, not me," without even thinking about it because our frenemy is so loud. We pigeonhole ourselves into being not *quite* enough. Not strong enough. Not vocal enough. Not smart enough. Not outgoing enough. Not bold enough. Not confident enough.

And then, guess what? We start to live within those limitations. We convince ourselves that because we don't feel 100 percent ready to conquer the challenge, we are not meant for greatness. That our personalities, our upbringing, and our past failures cannot be changed; thus, we live within the walls our frenemy builds for us.

And then we don't get asked again, which fuels our feelings of inadequacy. I see this often in the organizations and places in which I work.

"I asked her last year, and she said no. She said she wasn't interested," a well-meaning colleague explained when I suggested a woman for a job. I know her skills, expertise, and knowledge. I am confident she would be amazing in this position, and I know she would jump at the chance now. But because she didn't think she was the person for the job in the past, I have to try to convince him to ask her…again.

We must give ourselves permission to grow and accept that we can do things now that we may not have been ready to do before. It's perfectly acceptable to recognize when we have let our imposter phenomenon take over in the past, and change it moving forward.

It's also so important to recognize that even when we *do* fail, when we miss the mark, we don't have to let it feed the monster of insecurity, aka our frenemy. No rule states that our past mistakes are evidence of our future performances. Instead, we can take hold of our past failures and use them to fuel our confidence.

Wait, what? Stay with me. I promise you I have not been inhaling anesthesia gases. This will make sense in a minute.

I have failed. A lot. Big-time with big things. And I can tell you this: 99 percent of my internal growth and self-confidence have come as a result of my biggest failures. How I processed the failures, how I learned to let go of the shame associated with them, and how I allowed them to shape me, humble me, and make me brave have led to one singular truth: they have made me confident. Confident to pick myself up, confident to trust that God will meet me in whatever dire situation I find myself, confident that I will be better when I climb out of the pit. Confident that no matter what the challenge, I will survive it, even if it means I come out of the arena with horrific hair and looking like I slept on a park bench. Confident that no matter how strong my frenemy's voice is, I possess a much stronger voice that whispers, "You can do this, and doing it imperfectly is enough."

An Unforgiveable Failure

I want to share with you a tragic, horrible, true story. It is my story. If anyone ever told me that I would share it, let alone write about it, I would have been dumbstruck or gotten angry at even the suggestion. It is complicated, and as I write it, I cry. You see, I still feel significant sadness and grief about this story.

I always will.

I am sharing it because I have learned to let go of the shame that is associated with what for years I had convinced myself was my greatest failure, and mine alone. It involves human life and a beautiful family, whom I think of and pray for all the time. Even as I write it now, it is difficult to find the right words to bring honor to the death of a person whom God loved so deeply. I pray you are encouraged through this story.

Let me be completely clear: I am not alluding that I am in any way the victim. A precious family, who had to say good-bye to their loved one, suffered grief beyond anything I felt. While physicians may experience a phenomenon called "secondary victim phenomenon" because we often go through significant guilt, grief, and pain in silence, I by no means want to draw attention to myself with this story.[5] I do, however, want to pay my respects to this precious life. In doing so I hope to bring healing to others who have experienced similar outcomes.

A few years ago, I was a young attending anesthesiologist who was very skilled and secure in my training. Although I worked with a team of doctors, one night I was in charge of the anesthesia care of a critically ill patient who needed to go to the operating room for an urgent procedure. The patient was very ill and also very small. But the buck stopped with me. The surgery was extremely high risk, I had little backup, and the surgery outcome may not be good. But I was in charge, and I depended on my training and expertise.

Through a tragic series of events, the patient passed away in the operating room. I was devastated, crushed, and in utter grief. I had never lost a small person in the operating room, one with his entire life ahead of him. All I could think of was my own two small people at home, how much I loved them, and how I had let this family down. I blamed myself. I had failed to accomplish a life-saving effort that could have possibly saved this child.

I went home and was comatose. Something changed in me that day, and it has stayed with me every day since. I was a failure—in the worst way imaginable. A life was gone. A family was in mourning. And in my self-critical, young attending physician mind, I thought I could have prevented it. I couldn't see that I was part of a team, that the patient was critically ill, that the surgery was the highest risk of all surgeries, and that the patient suffered from diseases most likely none of us could treat.

It did not matter. None of those truths mattered. All that mattered was that I had failed, and a life was gone. The shame at times was unbearable. I walked around the hospital like a zombie for weeks, convinced people were standing in corners whispering about my failure that led to losing a life. Convinced I was worthless, I thought about quitting medicine, believing all of my years of studying and training were a mistake.

Over time my ability to work without fear improved marginally, but the shame never left me. A small child in the hospital would smile at me, and a flashback hit me. Emotions would overtake me so that I had to rush into the nearest bathroom and talk to myself to lower my heart rate. I would see a child being wheeled through the corridor, heading to receive treatment of some sort, and I experienced instant anxiety and immense panic. It was not until years later that I would realize I was suffering from post-traumatic stress disorder. I was wounded, injured, and convinced I was to blame.

During this time, my academic career in cardiac anesthesiology was successful and growing. I spoke at conferences, giving lectures around the country. The audiences became bigger and the talks more popular, but what no one knew was that inside, my frenemy was *screaming* at me, filling me with fear. It paralyzed me on the stage, especially once I was done speaking and the applause began. *Someone is going to come up to the microphone and call me out,* I would think, my heart racing. *They know about my failure, and they are going to tell everyone what I already know: I am a fraud, I am a terrible doctor, and I shouldn't be here. Maybe if I continue to do enough good, I will make up for my mistake. I must keep achieving to make up for this colossal failure.*

I lived like this for years, feeling as if at any time the scam would be up, and I would receive what I really deserved: shame, blame, and retribution. I punished myself internally for years. I didn't feel that I deserved to be happy, and I thought I had to achieve, achieve, achieve to cover up my past mistake. My brave husband knew every part of my failure and loved me through all my years of anxiety, shame, and self-berating. He sat quietly with me, holding my hand and telling me how proud he was of me. I couldn't accept his words. In my darkest hours, he never stopped building me up. Honestly, if he hadn't been there nonstop for me, I am very sure I would not have eventually found the healing I needed. He never told me to "get over it," and he never tried to fix me. He just kept loving me. Unconditionally.

I daily fed my imposter phenomenon with memories of this event, and I turned down several big opportunities that I believed would expose the "real me." I felt such deep remorse and failure, and although I asked thousands of times for God to forgive me, I could not forgive myself. This lasted seven years.

The Gift of Forgiveness

For my fortieth birthday, I took a much-needed vacation to a tropical location with my husband. I didn't want a big celebration. I craved only escape. What I really desired, though, was forgiveness...of myself. On a beach, thousands of miles from my home, I found it.

I often describe this experience as extraordinary, but, in reality, it was simply forgiveness. It was me facing my fears, seeing them objectively, working through the worst-case scenario that I had experienced, then letting go of the shame. It was me forgiving myself, refusing to feed my frenemy any more lies based on my past failure, and stepping out of the darkness I had cowered in for years.

My husband and I were sitting on the beach at the resort, reading books and enjoying the sun. An American couple was in the cabana next to us, also celebrating the wife's fortieth birthday. We struck up a conversation, eventually talking about vocations. He was a pastor, and much to our surprise, we realized we both knew some of the same people from our college days. My husband, Lance, had gone to college with a mutual friend of the pastor's wife. Lance and she took over the conversation.

After a few moments, Greg, the pastor, turned to me and asked a poignant question. "What do you love about being a doctor?"

Oh no. Here it comes. His harmless question revealed a deep sense of shame tied to my failure. My fear and anxiety bubbled to the surface as I struggled for my answer. As Brené Brown says, "When perfectionism is driving...shame is always riding shotgun."[6]

My frenemy's voice was so loud, it clouded my ability to even feel authentic answering the question. I loved being a doctor and could easily list why, but for some reason, I felt honesty boiling up in me. Perhaps because Greg and I shared the same faith. Maybe because it was time to face my demons. Possibly because I had had a margarita. It didn't matter why. It only mattered that it was time to come out with it.

I shared with this man and his wonderful wife how I loved practicing medicine, but that I couldn't let go of this one patient, whose grief I had carried with me every day as I failed to save this person's life. I shared with them how being a doctor wasn't all sunshine and roses, and while I loved it, I was by no means proud of my profession.

Pastor Greg didn't pass it off and ignore it. (Greg, if you are reading this, don't quit your day job.) This man was lounging on vacation, yet he *heard* me. While I was trying my best to be upbeat and positive, he heard the sadness and defeat in my voice, even though I wore a smile. He looked at me and said, "Can I pray for you? I would like to."

Standing on a beach in the middle of the ocean, a stranger prayed for me. He spoke wisdom over me. His words were simple yet profound. He asked God to remove the shame and guilt associated with my failure and to stop it from limiting my future. Even now as I type this, the reality of that moment is hard to explain. I can still hear the ocean and feel the tears on my face as I released all the guilt and shame associated with years of carrying this grief.

I realized how heavy the *perception* of my unforgivable failure was. The shame associated with it was like carrying around a ton of bricks. And at that moment, I released them. I did not plan on forgiving myself on a beach where I was trying to forget all my shortcomings and numb my pain. Yet somehow, in a moment, I was new.

I am not saying that letting go of our failures has to be a mountain-top experience with ocean waves and spiritual revelations. While I had been doing my best for years to work through this failure, my experience on the beach that day was simple yet powerful.

All the years I'd spent ruminating about what I could have done differently, a million "if onlys," suddenly were worth something. The person's life I failed to save was worth something all along, but only now did I allow it to mean what it should have meant from day one.

It was all worth something. All the pain and shame were forgiven, and I had to get to the point where someday I could help others by sharing this story. I had to be brave enough to share this experience—and my role in this failure—out loud with others. I had to share how hard it was to forgive myself, and I had to admit, finally, that I was not perfect. I would never be perfect, and I am okay just as I am. It was time to stop trying to achieve my way out of a past failure.

I can honestly tell you that if I had never experienced this release of shame, this book would not exist. The support group I lead for thousands of women physicians would not exist. The Brave Enough conferences, retreats, classes, and support groups would not be a reality.

The part I played in this tragic loss shaped me. Although I never wanted to discuss it for so many complex reasons, I must give credit to the truth: this tiny person who lost his precious life that day on my watch and whose face is etched in my mind forever has taught me so much.

When women share their brokenness with me, I grasp it. When doctors I train make mistakes and, in tears, share their grief, I understand it. When a patient's family grieves, I grieve with them. When someone tells me that she can't let go of her shame, I know she can.

Maybe you haven't experienced a failure like mine. Maybe you have. Perhaps your fear of failing feeds your imposter syndrome and is holding you back. Whatever the case, the above steps to overcoming work. I promise you, when you deal with your past failures, you will see yourself differently. The experiences you have gone through and survived will instill in you deep gratitude and a sense of respect.

You may never get to the place where you don't experience imposter syndrome, but you can definitely get to a point where you live without shame. You can grow to respect the past while also developing self-confidence and self-awareness. When you recognize imposter phenomenon for what it truly is, work through the steps to overcoming it. You will be amazed at what happens when you use them to your advantage.

Your frenemy loses her voice. Suddenly, you feel very comfortable living in the space between unbreakable grit and the immense grace that is needed to show up every day in your life. You find yourself living comfortably in the space of *Crap! I really screwed that up* and *I will do it better next time. I know I will.* You will smile when you look in the mirror and decide to love your body, despite the wrinkles, dimples, and imperfections. You will say yes to things that completely terrify you because you know growth lives there.

And more important, you find yourself forgiving. Forgiving others who require massive grace. Forgiving yourself, forgiving your enemies, and forgiving those who may not be sorry for the wrongs they committed.

Do the steps.

Dig deep.

Recognize the truths.

Forgive yourself.

And shut your frenemy up.

I bet you won't hear her anymore.

CHECKING IN WITH YOURSELF *Exercise 8*

Let's explore imposter syndrome and go inward to investigate your internal frenemy. Grab your journal and reflect on the following statements:

1) Have you ever been asked to do something you felt undeserving of? Did your thoughts make you turn down the opportunity? What was the role, and how did it feel to turn it down?

   _____

   _____

   _____

2) Now remove yourself from the circumstances and think of yourself as your friend. Objectively, what would your friend say to you? Be objective, as a friend. List your qualifications as you would talk to a friend.

   _____

   _____

   _____

3) Visualize yourself onstage, or about to perform; focus and meditate for five minutes on your successes. Think about all the work it took to make those successes a reality. Focus on the reasons you are in the position you are...that it is, indeed, due to your previous performance. Write them down.

   _____

_____

_____

4) Talk to a friend about your fears. Stating them out loud often makes them seem less significant and allows you to hear another person's perspective on your fears. Write down the positive results of facing your fears.

_____

_____

_____

The next time you are asked to do something, answer that you will think about it, even if you don't believe you are capable—and think about this exercise.

Chapter 9

Leadership and Lipstick

I am not going to limit myself
just because people won't accept the fact
that I can do something else.

—Dolly Parton[1]

You Don't Need More

 was angry. I had been in an important negotiation but left empty-handed. I had gone in prepared with impressive data and a good argument. As I lamented my frustration to a coworker, she interrupted. "Don't get upset about it. The guys wouldn't."

Of course, they wouldn't be upset, I thought. *Statistically, a man wouldn't have left empty-handed!* But I took her words to heart and thought about how I could have negotiated better, more like a man. After reading *Crucial Conversations* and other books on negotiating, I knew men were seen more favorably than women when negotiating.[2] Surely this meant that if I wanted a better outcome, I needed to model a man, right?

When I went into my next negotiation and tried to emulate a man, I felt ridiculous—unauthentic, rehearsed, and forced. I was incredibly direct, didn't mince words, and spoke more than I listened. I tried to be as flat and unswerving as possible. It makes me laugh at myself now as I tell this story, but this is what I had pictured a man would do: state forcefully why I deserved what I was asking for, as I had witnessed a few men do in prior meetings. Needless to say, my strategy didn't work, and I vowed that day never to negotiate, lead, speak, or teach in any way other than as myself. I should have gone into the negotiation with transparency, honesty, and facts. Now when I negotiate, I state at the beginning of the conversation, "Look, I am going to negotiate, and I know from the data that women are looked upon unfavorably and face backlash when they negotiate. I am telling you this now so that doesn't happen and we can both be as transparent as possible."

The path to success in the corporate world seems tailor-made for a man's walking shoes: the more assertive men are, the more competent they are judged to be. We know this is opposite for women, as the more assertive we are in the workplace, the more we face leadership backlash, as described in Chapter 2. Academia, science, and technology fields are similar, and we women receive societal cues that tell us to follow the path made for men. We struggle to follow the unwritten rules that tell us if we want to succeed professionally, we must alter our authentic selves or face backlash.

Some of us choose the latter. We rise up and fight the status quo, engaging in the workplace as our authentic selves. But we often find ourselves exhausted, constantly fighting the internal battle of who we truly are. And then what happens? We retreat. We grab the *man*-ual off the shelf and pick back up in chapter one. We grow war weary.

Some of us don't even realize we are following the *man*-ual. We are constantly conflicted in predominantly male environments and thus blame ourselves when we fail to get what we seek. We think we must not be strong enough, or we are too strong and stepped on toes, or it must be a personality flaw or blind spot we need to fix.

We operate in a constant flux of indecisiveness, unassured if we can step forward into roles or areas dominated by men. We think we just need a few more classes, more experience, and more mentorship. We blame ourselves for not arriving. We wonder why we were looked over, passed over, or told no. We assume we just need *more* of something.

I want to challenge the status quo on the notion that women need *more*. Actually, I want to flip the tables (except for the one I'll stand on) and shout this:

You do not need *more* classes, *more* of anything to strip yourself of being *you* and thus emulating men in the workplace to succeed. You *do* need opportunities to grow, strong mentors to follow, and sponsorships to open doors for you so you can learn from your failures and wins *as a woman*.

You will become the best *you* by growing within experiences and roles. One of the loudest messages we women hear in the workplace is that if we think like a man, we think like a leader. No, no, no! *Did you hear me?!* (Sorry if you haven't had coffee yet.)

We are not men. Many men have great attributes and make great leaders. But it is not because they are men. It is because they are wise people, servant-minded, strategic thinkers, and have strong work ethics. Guess what? Strong women leaders possess those same attributes but display them in different ways. Women are communal, great listeners, strategic thinkers, and also have incredibly strong work ethics.

Leaders with these attributes are what make organizations strong! There is room at the table for *both* men's and women's ideas. We are not the same but are wonderfully different. God created each human being with a specific set of strengths, creativity, and diversity that is radically and desperately needed within our organizations and workplaces. We must unlink the concept of men and women competing against one another in the workplace. We must embrace our differences and celebrate the distinctive qualities and abilities we each possess.

Men and women were created differently for a reason, and our differences *are our strengths*. When we lead as women, we may lead contrarily than our male colleagues, and that's a worthy thing. Research has shown that diverse thinking is great for innovation and for teams.[3] Fortune 500 companies that have diverse boards, made up of both men and women, not only have more innovation but also demonstrate better financial growth and return on investment.

When we come together as diverse people, we see things differently, we hear things in ways others may not, and, thus, we may identify groups of people or important concerns that would otherwise go unnoticed.

Leading as a Woman

To lead as strong women, we must embrace the fact that we *are* women. We need to stop hiding our mix of attributes, both feminine and masculine—the special sauce that makes us unique individuals. We must recognize that women shouldn't be expected to model themselves after their male colleagues; rather, we should strive to emulate character aspects of their leadership strengths, while acknowledging the way we express those attributes will be unique and much different.

When we understand our internal conflict and stress, we recognize it is often from two things:

1) The result of living inauthentically
2) The backlash of living authentically

This allows us to address solutions we so desperately need to keep fighting the good fight.

Recognizing that we may experience internal conflict when expressing our strengths as women and understanding what it means to thrive in a world in which we are not the elevated gender requires *clarity*. Clarity requires time alone with ourselves to come to these truths. Therefore, one of the most important gifts we can give ourselves is time. We need time alone to process our own authenticity, who God made us to be, and our own power and limitations.

The Power of Time Alone

Time alone to pour into our authenticity is often referred to as *self-care*. I like to call it *internal work* because, quite frankly, it isn't easy. It's how I feed my soul, identify my weaknesses, process my failures, and reset my mental health. It is work.

Time with ourselves is the single most difficult thing we women seem to be able to find these days. It's a hot commodity, like finding a Gucci bag discounted in T.J. Maxx. We convince ourselves that time alone is optional, like dessert. We view it as a luxury, not a necessity. We label it as selfish, and shame one another when learning one of us has taken time for ourselves.

"Wow, Nicole has time to run every day? What a luxury!" "Did you know that Tara gets a massage every other week? I have no idea how she finds the time." This is our judgment even though we are drowning in life and could benefit from just such self-care. "Did you know that Beth goes to a Bible study each week? Can you imagine?" we gripe to our equally exhausted colleagues.

We women actually exalt martyrdom. We celebrate women who look and feel as haggard as we are with comments like, "Oh, I haven't been to the doctor in years. What, you got a pedicure? Must be nice." And so on.

Are you laughing? It's true, isn't it? I know these things, sisters, only because I am at fault for falling into this critical-thinking error. When we see a woman taking time for herself, we become, well, jealous. Jealousy says, "Why does she get to make herself a priority?" "Why does she allow herself time for filling her soul?" But our jealously is revealing what we are really thinking: *Why don't I do this? Why don't I believe I am worth taking time to work on myself, my mental and physical well-being, and my personal development? Aren't I worth it?*

What I really want to say to you in this chapter is this:

1) Authenticity, and living as a woman in this world, requires doing internal work.
2) Internal work is self-care.

3) Self-care requires time and the acknowledgment that no one is
   going to take care of *you but you.*

We women are accustomed to putting everyone else first: our families,
our friends, our work, and our colleagues. We are applauded for having
beautifully structured homes and happy families. We feel pressure to be
Pinterest moms and craft queens. We are expected to stay a size six and
bring organic homemade snacks to soccer games, all while managing
successful careers. No one faults us for putting our families first and our
careers second. But what happens is we put our own care last, and our
authenticity goes out the window.

I want to talk for a moment about the happiness-versus-opportunity
paradox that Generation X women face in our society. While in many
ways we see women on the rise and an increasing number of opportunities
opening for women, we are, in general, becoming progressively less well.
Several studies have looked at women's well-being in the last decade, and
the data suggest that compared with men's overall well-being, the well-
being of women is on the decline.

A study conducted over a span of thirty-five years by Stevenson and
Wolfers from the General Social Survey in 2009 compared the general wellness of women with men and revealed that women report less happiness and
well-being compared with men.[4] When the researchers surveyed thousands
of American women and asked them general questions about their overall
financial health, relationships, job satisfaction, and well-being and happiness, they found that women reported being less satisfied and less well with
each subsequent decade. The overall results: men reported improvements
in well-being, while women reported declines in the same period. Studies
also show that over a quarter of women (26 percent) in America are taking
antidepressants compared with 21 percent a decade earlier.[5]

Why is this happening? Why are women gaining in some aspects of gender parity but reporting less life satisfaction? Why are we slowly seeing more women assume leadership roles but simultaneously burn out, report dissatisfaction with life, and become less well?

It is because we have not let go of the *man*-ual. We are still trying to live by the rule, "This is how you do the job well—by emulating men." While we deserve to step into roles and expectations that we can certainly fulfill, we are not stepping out of expectations others place on us to do all the things. We do our best to live as women all the while leading as men.

It is exhausting. It is depleting. I've had enough. Have you? We are constantly aware of others' expectations of us: we must lead, show no weakness, be ever present and ever available for all in our workplaces, while also being there for everyone at home.

We have stepped into spaces not previously occupied by women, but here is the thing: we are women. It is who we are, it is our being, and it is our identity. We lead differently, feel differently, and process stress and failure differently from men. And we must be able to do so authentically, *as women*. The only way women will be able to continually advance is to do so authentically. Let's pause and focus on that for a minute.

We must accept the fact that our roles in and out of the workplace will be different from our male colleagues, and that is perfectly all right and acceptable.

> *"Your time is limited,*
> *so don't waste it*
> *living someone else's life."*
>
> —Steve Jobs

The reality, however, is that we must accept that being a woman who wants to succeed in a male environment comes with a set of challenges that are complex and discouraging at times, and it requires energy and focus.

We must also accept that this is okay and that we can and will face these challenges, and we can overcome them. We must understand that many of us are caregivers and life givers. Over the phone we can put out a fire between two squabbling teens one minute and deliver to the board a million-dollar budget proposal the next. It's what leadership looks like in a woman.

We must accept that while working in a hospital, we can cheer via FaceTime with the toddler who just pooped in the potty for the first time and then hang up and run a code on a dying person. It's what leadership looks like in a woman.

We must accept that we can cry over coffee with our work colleague who just made a huge mistake and encourage her, then walk into a boardroom and present a new educational model to our team. It's what leadership looks like in a woman.

We must accept that four-inch heels belong on the stage next to the suits and ties, and when we deliver the keynote to a standing ovation, we may be wearing red lipstick. It's what leadership looks like in a woman.

We must accept that if you interrupt us in a meeting or take credit for our idea, we will confront you head-on and not tolerate it anymore, no matter how uncomfortable you feel. It's what leadership looks like in a woman.

We must accept that if you ask us to take on more work, we expect to be paid for it, as you would pay a man. It's what leadership looks like in a woman.

How do we do this? How do we thrive in our lives as women, accepting our unique strengths and weaknesses and showing up anyway? How do we give ourselves time to grow into the people we were supposed to be all along?

EACH OF YOU RIGHT NOW TAKE A DEEP, CLEANSING BREATH.
Feel it. To your toes. Wherever you are, quiet your mind and turn off all distractions. Close your eyes, and focus.

Say these affirming words out loud, to yourself:

I am a woman, and I am enough.

I can lead as a woman.

I can grow as a woman.

I am permitted to fail and learn from my mistakes as a woman.

I am permitted to speak up, even if I am scared, as a woman.

I belong as a woman.

Any obstacle I face, I am not alone.

I belong to a tribe, and women who have come before me overcame similar struggles.

I was made by a Creator, and I can face the next challenge as a woman.

I will give myself time and value myself as a created human on this earth.

But First: Remove

Let's break it down. Before we can dive into *adding* self-care and internal work, we have to address the process of *removing* responsibilities and duties on your plate that don't need you anymore. That's right: removing. We live in a world in which we receive nonstop messages of what we "need" to add to our lives. Do more yoga! Add more protein! Read more books! Attend more conferences! Get Botox! Subscribe to this channel!

I promised myself when I wrote this book that I would encourage you in ways that are realistic and applicable to the woman like you, who is trying to make it to work each day with matching shoes, to clean out the veggie drawer at least once a year, and not to accidentally forget a child on a soccer field (been there, done that). So if I am saying that you need to add in some time for internal work and self-care, I am also going to help you remove something.

Lord knows, if you have a free hour in your day to devote to yourself, you sure as heck don't need any more grit or grace. You may, however, need strong legal advice or an escape plan because this available hour might mean you are imprisoned or being held against your will.

I'm guessing you don't have that free hour. So the first step to creating time for yourself is to make what I call an "outlist." What activities or obligations that you do not enjoy can you let go of? These may be domestic duties, work duties, or volunteer duties. We often have this false belief that all women everywhere must do everything. Perhaps someone told us it is our duty, or we tell ourselves that life is hard and we can't ask for help, so we convince ourselves that we must do what doesn't bring us joy.

Why can't we ask for help? It's silly, and, quite frankly, arrogant to think we women can do it all. The fact is, we can't. We aren't superhuman; we are human. We women need to take one big collective breath and say, "It is okay to ask for help."

Let's do an outlist. Look into tasks and activities you can let go of that don't bring you joy:

- Cleaning and laundry
- Home organization
- Meal preparation
- Errands and grocery shopping
- Committee work
- Extra shifts
- Citizenship duties
- Volunteering

Before you start to riot, if these items fill your heart and bring you peace, by all means, do them! But if you've listed some tasks that you don't love, please ask for help. You are allowed to ask for help. You are allowed to outsource.

You are also allowed to say no. Did you know that no is a complete sentence? Saying no to activities you don't have time for (even if you love them) is a skill that requires constant practice.

Setting Boundaries

Here's the thing: people don't ask you to do things unless they know you will say yes. So don't fall into the trap of thinking you must say yes if someone asks to do something. Take it as a compliment that you were asked, and then say no, thank you. You do not need to explain why you said no. You do not need to apologize for saying no. As someone wise once said, "You are not required to set yourself on fire to keep everyone else warm."

I hear women often say, "I am sorry, but I can't do that." Why are you sorry? Did you just accidentally trip an elderly person or stab your frenemy with a steak knife? Those are things you apologize for. You do not, by any means, need to apologize for keeping yourself sane.

You do not, for any reason, need to apologize for giving yourself grace and space. You do not need to apologize for devising an outlist and removing things from your life that drain you or are an overcommitment of your time. One of the most empowering acts you can do for yourself is to set boundaries. Learn to say no to people, unapologetically. Be your own CEO. Why is this important? Because when you say "No, thank you," people realize that you are comfortable with leading as a woman.

When you say, "I can't do that for you because it's not best for me," people around you take notice. They realize you are the CEO of your life, and you are brave enough to say what is best for you and your own well-being. While others may become frustrated at you for sticking to your boundaries, or even angry, it is important to know this may happen and not detour. There is power in saying no and in setting healthy boundaries. You allow yourself to be the unique person God made you to be and to give yourself time to work on the areas in your life that need attention.

I hear women also say, "I wish I had more time to learn that," or "I wish I had time to exercise," or "I wish I had time to read." Guess what? You do. You make time for your priorities. If you do not have time for yourself, you are saying, "I am not a priority. Everyone else is."

I understand this battle because I face it daily. I am constantly having to work on the responsibility creep: I tend to say yes because I'm too tired to say no, which results in allowing others to dictate my life for me.

I am also guilty of saying yes to things I don't love or have time to do because someone asked me nicely. I've learned that just because someone asks me in a pretty package, the answer is still no. Lately, I have been thinking this way when others ask me nicely: Would I get into the back of a white van if the male driver asked me nicely?

Exactly.

Think of the person who asks you to do something you don't have time for as a strange man in a suspicious white van. Make it a *heck no* and run in the other direction! This approach may seem a little dramatic, but I say whatever it takes, sister. Learning to care for yourself, first and foremost, is not an easy task. It takes practice to remove tasks that quietly creep in and threaten to overtake the boundaries you set for yourself. If we want to thrive, we must own that our lives and health are our most precious commodities.

Unless the request makes you jump with pure glee, it is a *no*. Unless you've been waiting to take on this extra task for a lifetime, it is a *no*.

It may seem counterintuitive to invest in yourself when you're leading others, but the truth is, the more successful you become, the greater the stress you will likely experience. The more responsibilities you have in life, the more important it is to be resilient and well. One of the hallmarks of resiliency is the ability to practice self-care and self-reflection, both of which require time.

I want to challenge you to give yourself what I call an "hour of power." It can be meditation, reading Scripture, yoga, exercise, time with friends, writing, taking a long walk, or savoring your favorite music or a glass of wine. The truth is, the hour of power is different for each and every person. When women understand the importance of self-care and put their own health and well-being first, they become courageous. They give themselves grace. Then bravery and grit develop and strengthen, building them into the woman they were meant to be all along.

INTERNAL CHECK:

Your Hour of Power

If I asked you to look for one hour in your day to spend on self-care, where would you find it? You would probably cut out an hour of sleep, which is not healthy. You need all the sleep you can get. So let's start simple: one hour a day is 4 percent of your day. If we cut that in half to thirty minutes, that is 2 percent. You deserve 2 percent of your day. It's not an option. So let's find it.

Step 1. Think of some activity or task you can remove. What can you remove that will open up thirty minutes of your day?

Step 2. On Sunday, plan your thirty minutes for each day of the week. Recognize this is a change, but challenge yourself to follow through. Unplug by yourself during these thirty minutes. Journal, exercise, take a walk, stretch. Write something, perhaps a letter to an old friend. Create. Play music. Spend time on your inner self. You will be amazed at how thirty minutes a day spent on yourself can make you resilient and brave.

Step 3. Tell those in your life (family, coworkers, children, spouse) who may be influenced by this new boundary about your plan for self-care. Embrace it, and commit to it.

When we spend time with our internal selves and take care of our minds and bodies, we feel more comfortable being who we were made to be. The direct result of self-care and time alone is embracing our authenticity.

Personally, I have to do my hour of power first thing in the morning. I force myself to wake up and spend thirty minutes to an hour on my health: spiritual, physical, and mental. Sometimes I read Scripture. Other times I lift weights. Sometimes I row. At times I write in my journal. Or I sit at the island in the kitchen in the dark with a cup of coffee and weep. For reals.

My hour of power is like a gift to myself. I allow myself to think about something other than my to-do list or my inbox. I allow myself to grieve, to dream, to feel joy and pride. I allow myself to be Sasha.

I want to encourage you, dear sister, to give yourself this time. If there is one thing I hope to hear someday, it is that this book gave you permission to invest in you. That after reading this book you were brave enough to remove some tasks, which then allowed you to prioritize self-care in your life. That you engaged in doing the internal work from which you gained the insight to live more authentically.

When I look back over my life, I can definitely see trends in my self-development. There were seasons when I felt I was trying to run in quicksand, making the same mistakes over and over. It was during these times that I beat myself up for never quite reaching the magical level of ultimate work-life balance and failing to live up to the fantasy Instagram-worthy dream world in which my family is perfect, my home is pristine, and on most days I like myself.

Looking in the rearview mirror of my life, I also saw times when I felt on top of the world, as if all the pistons of my life, my family, my work, and my health were in sync.

But the truth is, we don't live on mountain tops. We live in a world of ebb and flow, of challenges and difficulties intermixed with joyous celebrations and amazing victories. We live in a world of cancer and finishing marathons, cellulite and squeezing into our favorite jeans. We live in a world of the best romance ever, coupled with divorce and betrayal. We live in a real world, one without filters and autocorrect, of hurting others and being hurt ourselves, of loyalty and loss. Of grit and grace.

Sometimes we just don't feel like showing up. We don't want to be the women we know we are capable of being. We want to stay in bed, pull the covers over our heads, and ignore the small human asking us for pancakes or the large human asking us if we've seen his keys. We don't want to deal with our messy, imperfect lives.

Thank goodness we show up anyway. Thank goodness we help patients even when we are tired ourselves, we stop and listen to our friends even when we don't think we have much to offer, and we help little people who need us to calm their fears at three in the morning when we haven't slept through the night in a year. Thank goodness we are gritty. Thank goodness we show grace.

In the messy yet beautiful ups and downs of life, time with ourselves keeps us grounded. Doing the internal work allows us to give grace to others through forgiveness and possess the grit needed to forge ahead to the next challenge. Routine time with ourselves to dive deep allows us to lead as women and thrive in doing so. We become settled in who we are, we understand our strengths and our weaknesses, and we give ourselves space to process the challenges that life throws at us.

Have you ever come home angry, and without cause snapped at your partner, your kids, or even your pet? Take a walk. A short, ten-minute walk alone, sorting out your anger and realizing that your emotions don't have to hijack your actions, is self-care.

Have you ever woken up in the morning and dreaded your workday, thinking of ways to avoid going into the office? Get up, stretch, make a cup of coffee, and read a little bit. Write in your journal a daily affirmation of how you are going to be grateful. Determine what attitude *you* will set as well as the outcome of your day's events.

Have you ever come home overwhelmed and devoured a bag of cookies, only to feel like a walking marshmallow immediately after? Next time try taking a hot bath. Close your eyes and meditate on your favorite things, even if it's for fifteen minutes. Release your negative thoughts, and mentally list all of the ways you are blessed.

We are allowed to ask for help. We are allowed to stop and care for ourselves. Self-reflection and taking time to do the internal work has many benefits. Instead of collapsing in a chair with a bag of carbs and watching Netflix, allow yourself to be alone and process your thoughts. It is amazing how much this has helped me work through negative emotions and stressful thoughts from my day, instead of projecting them into my next interaction or the following day. Releasing stress from our minds is an active process. While it seems much easier to numb our thoughts with food or negative behaviors, it is much healthier when we do the hard internal work of allowing ourselves to feel and process each thought and emotion.

A woman is wise who utilizes her strengths and refuels her tank when she feels empty. It not only is okay to ask for help, it is critical to our well-being and success. Maybe you don't consider yourself a leader, but I challenge you on this thought. You are your *own* leader, and you make the agenda in your life and choices that determine your well-being.

Many times we say yes to what does not align with our passions, or we stay in the comfort of the known, afraid to embrace those desires that seem out of reach. When we spend time with our thoughts on self-care, we discover our strengths. We dream a little; we think big. We allow ourselves to say yes to our goals and no to anything that doesn't bring us joy and peace. We let go of others' expectations of us and the guilt that hangs around our necks. When we know our passions, we know what it means to be truly ourselves. This is the pathway to living our most authentic lives. This is living brave enough.

CHECKING IN WITH YOURSELF *Exercise 9*

Let's find your Hour of Power and commit to developing self-care. Grab your journal and reflect on the following statements and questions:

1) List the ways you recharge. Perhaps it is an hour of exercise or coffee with a friend. Try to tease out the difference between decompressing (activities that remove the dirty water from your cup) and recharging (activities that refill your cup with fresh water).

   _____

   _____

   _____

2) Think of ways that allow you to lead, work, and live authentically as a woman. List what those are for you. For example, maybe you love to write. How can you make writing part of your career responsibilities? What is your favorite hobby or skill that you have always wanted to do? Maybe it is painting, ballroom dancing, or traveling. What is one challenge at work that you would love to find the solution to but feel you aren't qualified to do? Have you ever told your boss what your dream job entails? Do you hide these desires, downplaying them or making them appear less important to you? Why?

   _____

   _____

   _____

3) Schedule time in the next month to invest in authentic self-care. Think about which of these activities can be routine rather than once-a-year events. Think about what you may need to remove from your week for these activities to happen.

_____

_____

_____

Chapter 10

The Safety of the Shore

I come as one, but I stand
as 10,000.

—*Maya Angelou*[1]

The Rise of the Strong Woman

D eb Gilg is a brilliant lawyer who has served as a U.S. Attorney. The first time I met her, she was speaking to a group of professional women. I sat in the audience, brimming with excitement to hear her story. She was a powerful force, full of confidence, and yet she exuded compelling warmth and beauty. I had read her bio beforehand and knew that her honors, successes, and career were impressive. She was a high achiever. I was eager to hear how she had done it all. What was her secret? What could I learn from her?

From her first words, the entire room fell silent. The first sentence out of her mouth was shocking. She calmly described an abusive childhood. She repeated with ease the things her alcoholic father had told her over and over: "You're not smart." "You're not pretty." "You will never amount to anything."

But then she said something I will never forget. "But my grandfather would whisper the opposite things to me. He would say, 'You're smart.' Or, 'You'd better get a good grade on your math test because you are going to be something someday.' And for some reason, it was his voice that carried me."

Tears welled in my eyes. I sat there stunned. She went on to talk about her work, her career, and all she had accomplished. But I couldn't get past one thing: the words she *chose* to listen to allowed her to be brave enough to be her real self. What made her choose to listen to her grandfather's voice and not her father's? What made her decide she was worthy, she was smart, and she was more than the sum of her father's criticism? What caused her to tune out the voices of despair and negativity and listen to the steady voice that whispered, "You can"?

I thought about Deb's decision to listen to the positive voice. I thought about the times I had allowed negative voices and criticism to drown out the positive voices. I considered how words spoken to me by naysayers undercut me to my core. I have replayed those voices in my head over and over, like a favorite song. I have let the beliefs of others, and their esteem of me, change my course. I have allowed the words of others to become part of my own internal voice.

It took me nearly forty years to recognize the need to remove from my internal dialogue the negative voices and untruths others said about me or to me. I had to make a conscious effort to identify what I believed about myself based on what others told me. Here's the thing about criticism and harshness: even if I knew they weren't "all" true, a wee bit of *maybe* was tucked in them, casting doubt into my confidence and ability to trust myself.

We take these untruths off the rack and hold them up against us as we peer into the mirror as if shopping for a new outfit and wondering if this will fit or how we'll look in it. Will this one work? *Hmmm,* maybe. We invite these negative thoughts in, welcoming them to stay for a while as we treat them to snacks and pour them a fresh cup of coffee.

Throughout my twenties and thirties, I made decisions based on what others told me I was or wasn't good at. Even though I was still discovering my strengths and weaknesses, I often believed what others told me about myself, even if they didn't have my best interests in mind. I hushed the voice that said, "You can," or "You just haven't figured that out *yet.*" Instead of speaking up, instead of following my dreams, I tried to overachieve in the areas I knew I was good at. There were times my fear paralyzed me. It stopped me from cultivating a life of richness and fullness because I was too afraid to try new things. If I didn't think I would be great at something, if I thought I was weak in an area, I wouldn't pursue it. I ignored areas of weakness that would have benefited from me working on them, and instead, overachieved in areas of my strengths.

Choosing Empowered

Oftentimes we come to a fork in the road. It may be an opportunity we are offered, or when we want to assert our self-confidence and say, "No, I am not taking that path anymore. I am going this way." We feel a bolt of confidence, a shot of authenticity welling up inside of us. We choose to listen to the right voice, the one that says "You *can*—you just haven't *yet*." We adopt a growth mind-set and believe any backlash we may face will be worth it. We stand stronger and speak the words we hear in our heads. We take the path less traveled by women, the one full of weeds and thick undergrowth. The one that is harder but quieter. The path of brave. The path of us.

When we are brave enough to live authentically, we are brave enough to accept our value. We begin to live as if we, our lives, our opinions, and our unique gifts, matter. Something critical inside of us changes. An internal shift occurs. We may not be able to pinpoint it to one moment or a single interaction; rather, it is a gradual alteration of our selves. Then one day we look behind us and note that we are far past the tipping point, and we are becoming. We like who God created us to be a little more. We appreciate our strengths, and we show ourselves grace for our weaknesses.

Each day we live in a space of increasing grit and grace. We stand straighter and speak with authority because we are *empowered*. Instead of apologizing, we say thank you. Instead of shrinking and hiding, we show up. Instead of allowing fear to stop us, we step forward, wrapping our fear in courage. Instead of living in others' expectations, we claim our own boundaries. Instead of convincing ourselves we aren't good enough, we celebrate who we are now.

I want to stress a realization that came to me as I accepted that I could be gritty and show grace. These two attributes, which for so long I separated in my mind as arch enemies or rivals, were indeed a pairing of a successful life. It changed my future, and I hope it will change yours.

We women grow up associating confidence and the ability to give orders as masculine. We are taught that being a woman equals being obedient, raising our hands, and asking permission. We are hesitant to defend our own boundaries and set our own agendas as we don't want to offend people, especially those we love and respect. We are communal, collaborators, and connectors. The majority of us want to help others, and we love seeing other people succeed. Add these together and it's a recipe for over-committed, undervalued, and completely exhausted women. As discussed earlier, it is ingrained in us as children: women are givers. And we give and give and give…until we fall apart.

If you want to be the best version of you, you have to spend time on the inside. You must evaluate your boundaries, review your priorities, and ask yourself some tough questions. You can do all of these things, but if you don't believe you are empowered to make necessary changes, you will continue to burn for others until there is nothing left of you.

How do we become empowered? How do we believe we can make the changes necessary to live authentically, to set boundaries, to embrace being gritty and showing grace? Is there a class we can take? A program we can sign up for? Earn a certificate maybe?

Maybe the trick is losing ten pounds. Maybe we will be more empowered if we get Botox. Maybe one day we will unlock our inner Super-woman, and suddenly everyone will respect our boundaries and accept us for who we are. If only we could look younger, run a faster mile, or read 100 self-help books. We just need to get rid of our laugh lines or get some lowlights. Or maybe we need to start our days with a kale smoothie and eat more plants! That's it! We will arrive, and all will obey our commands. We will never be uncomfortable or face backlash being our true selves if we start our day with spinach.

Lord, have mercy and send help to Your people.

Living Empowered Is Living Loved

Here is what I have learned and know to be true: living authentically is determined by a choice only *you* can make. You will live authentically only when you believe you are empowered because you are a human. Not because you are a woman, not because you are a man, not because you are a mother or a wife or a doctor or a lawyer or anything else. You will believe this when you believe you were created empowered—because you are loved.

You will set boundaries and live authentically—speaking up, standing straighter, leading, living—because you are loved and you are enough. Your worth is in the fact that you are *here*. You were created by One who knit you together—perfectly imperfect, a beautiful tapestry of both masculine and feminine traits of grit and grace. I do not believe success breeds authenticity. I believe authenticity breeds success.

I do not believe being empowered has anything to do with actually being *in power*. I believe that when we are brave enough to live empowered, we claim authority over ourselves, independent of our positions in our careers. It is not about being in control over others; it is about being empowered to set our lives' boundaries that represent our lives' priorities. It is showing up in our workplaces, our relationships, and our struggles and saying, "This is me. I am strong, I am gritty. I am imperfect, and I can show grace. I am empowered because I am loved. I am loved because I was created uniquely and sufficiently."

I used to begin difficult conversations with "I am sorry." Those three words started each and every conversation in which I had to disappoint someone who had either asked me to do a task or assumed I would. When I had to tell someone that I was choosing no longer to work for free or to continue a task that was someone else's responsibility, I apologized profusely. "I am sorry I can't do this task for free anymore," or "I am sorry but I don't have time for this job that really isn't my responsibility." I winced as I apologized. What I was really saying was, "I am sorry for setting boundaries and respecting myself. I am sorry for demanding compensation for my work and thus for all women's work. I am sorry for protecting my sanity and well-being."

Over time, after I burned out and spent time in the pit, I recognized that I was empowered. I realized that as CEO of my own time, my power was sitting on a shelf waiting for me to grasp it. My ability to live empowered was not a magic pill hidden in size eight jeans or in a cucumber smoothie. And guess what happened? *I stopped apologizing.*

HERE ARE SOME EXAMPLES:

I had assumed responsibilities at work that required a large amount of effort and with no compensation. I approached my boss and asked to be paid. I struggled not to apologize for asking. Why was I even considering apologizing for what was rightfully mine? I realized that in no way, shape, or form could I apologize for asking for what I was worth.

I was invited to speak at a gathering. I accepted. After I had accepted, the organizers asked me to speak on another topic, which would require me to lengthen my stay, with no extra compensation. I respectfully declined, saying, "I am sorry, but I must return home." Why did I apologize for setting healthy boundaries? I stopped apologizing for protecting my time.

When I began speaking and writing about women issues, a male colleague sidebarred me. While his intent was good, he told me that to "dabble" in gender issues would be a "career killer" and suggested I stick to medical-related topics and avoid social media or writing on "soft" issues. I said, "I am sorry, but I feel passionate about helping women." Why was I apologizing for refusing to live someone else's expectation of me? I stopped immediately.

I once walked onto the stage at a national meeting to give a talk. I introduced myself to my all-male copresenters. One of the well-known men speaking on the panel said, "Ah, Dr. Shillcutt, we know why you were asked to speak on this panel. There are *two* reasons," and nodded at my breasts. As the others stared at me, I turned every shade of red as my heart pounded. I was about to give a speech in front of hundreds of my peers. I fumbled and said something to the effect of, "I'm sorry, excuse me. I need to prepare for my talk," and hurried to my seat on the stage. Why was I apologizing for someone's inappropriate comments and bias against me? After I debriefed later with my husband, I vowed I would never, ever apologize for someone else's sexist comments. Now I say, "Can you repeat that?" and throw garbage right back where it came from.

Have you ever received negative feedback for putting your health or self-care above your work? Have you ever tried to hide from a coworker with regard to your upcoming vacation, exercise routine, or day off because you felt guilty recharging and replenishing your well-being? I have. I have found myself typing in emails, "I am sorry, but

I am on vacation that day." Why was I apologizing for protecting my own well-being? It required some effort, but I worked at being aware of when I would write or say I was sorry for simply taking the time to be a better me.

One time a leader I greatly respected asked me, "Sasha, what is this Brave Enough thing? Is this a midlife crisis?" I swallowed hard. I did not want to let him down. I deeply respected this man. I began my explanation with an apology, that I was sorry to tell him, but I actually really enjoyed empowering women. I felt it was my life mission to encourage women who were struggling with being themselves and facing constant criticism and bias in the workplace. Later, I still felt somehow like I had let him down. I realize now that I should never apologize for what I know God has called me to do. Why was I apologizing for pursuing my own life mission and passion?

Getting Comfortable with Being Uncomfortable

I flipped the switch. I took the power off the shelf and started using it. Now I start off crucial or difficult conversations in which I am going to say, "No, thank you," from a position of power. My own power. You see, when you start a conversation with "I am sorry," you start from a place of *beneath*. Starting with an apology places the context of your following words in the realm of "I messed up" and "I let you down" and "I am not doing what I am supposed to do." It is a losing position, and you do not belong there. You are not a loser.

Empowered to live your own authenticity, you start off conversations with a thank-you. You replace apologies with gratitude. Speaking from a place of empowerment, you are thankful for the opportunity, not sorry you can't commit. You are thankful you were asked and thankful you were considered, not sorry. You are demonstrating to others where your boundaries are. As you do this, you are educating them. You don't shrink and become smaller with apologies; rather, you educate by saying, "Thank you, but this isn't best for me."

Do you see how the conversation will proceed differently? When we believe we are worthy and that we are enough, we speak from a place of empowerment. Just because something conveniences someone else doesn't mean we must say yes.

The very opposite is also true. When we rise to the place in our lives when we know we must do *that thing*—asking for the compensation we deserve, negotiating a different time split, or requesting the position or promotion we want may be an uncomfortable conversation—it will bring feelings of unease to both ourselves and others. It may inconvenience someone else to say *yes* to us.

Most of the time, when we say no to someone else, we are, in turn, saying yes to the very thing we want for our own lives, and it is unfamiliar, even difficult. Getting comfortable being uncomfortable is required if we want to live authentically. If we want to exert courage, set boundaries, and live empowered, we won't win Miss Congeniality contests. Living empowered means having routine conversations with people who will try to enforce their wills on us. We will have to say (sometimes over and over), "No, and thank you."

We will likely need to have these conversations with people we love and respect. It is easy to say no, thank you to people we wish we could vote off the island. It is much harder to say, "This is who I am, and what you are asking me to do isn't a part of me," to people we love or those whose love we want.

Let that sink in for a minute. It's important because it is one of the critical steps to being comfortable with the uncomfortable, one of the hallmarks of living authentically. When you have internal conflict because you are speaking from a place of empowerment, ask yourself why. Is it because you don't believe you are empowered, or is it because you simply want to be liked?

When we come into a crucial conversation from a place of ego, wanting to receive lots of "atta girls" and flattery, approval, or warm fuzzies, we are feeding our internal need for attention and admiration. It is easy to cover this under a blanket of "wanting to help others," but we sensationalize being a martyr, which feeds our egos. We fail to protect our well-being, authenticity, and what we know we are called to do because it feels better to be liked than it does to be respected.

I promise you, dear sister, it is much better to be respected than it is to be liked. Being liked may seem easier, but in the long run, it is draining, exhausting, and equivalent to searching for the holy grail of interpersonal satisfaction. The more you try to please everyone, the more you will find it impossible. In the end, you will wear so many masks you don't remember your natural hair color. Was it brown with hints of red? Honey blonde? Jet black? We don't know. Better start over.

When you live empowered and grant yourself the autonomy of living authentically, you set healthy boundaries. You show up to work on your terms. You know your passion, your goals, and what you simply won't or don't do anymore. You know what brings you joy and what brings you down. You disengage from people and places that drain you. People in your life will take notice. They will respect you and the boundaries you set. It's like you've hung a shingle on your life that says EMPOWERED and the hours you're open for business.

It does not mean you won't continue to struggle with finding your internal positive voice. It doesn't mean you won't ever doubt yourself or your purpose in life. It does mean that when you are in those dark periods or when you feel alone and completely blind, you will cling to the hope you know to be true.

Just Enough Brave

I couldn't write a chapter about living brave without telling you about a very dark period in my life when I learned how to be brave enough. Not brave but brave *enough*. Just *enough* brave to get through the day...and the next. It was a time when each morning I lay in bed at 4:30 AM and thought, *Where will I get the courage to get through this day? I don't have any brave left. Please God, can I borrow some of Yours?*

It was a hard time in my life mostly because I had to be quiet. I had to hold all of my fears inside, feelings of complete despair, anxiety, and self-doubt. As an extrovert, I want to tell the world my feelings, both joyful and sorrowful. I like to talk through difficult scenarios with my close friends and ask them to weigh in. It's in my DNA to send out a survey to my tribe and ask "What would you do?" I am constantly seeking input from others and listening to others' opinions on my life. It's therapeutic for me to hear from my people.

It's very, very difficult for me to stay silent, especially during times of hardship. But I can tell you, I learned how to be just enough brave...when I remained silent. When I went inward and kept my thoughts and feelings known to God and my husband alone.

Have you ever experienced a time when you felt completely alone? You were so isolated and your thoughts and worries were so secluded that you felt as if any moment you would disappear. "What happened to her?" "We didn't even know she was struggling," you imagine people saying as you drift away. I have been there. I have faced a giant. I have felt like David, with Goliath roaring "DAVID," and the earth disappearing, leaving me completely alone, with no breath in me.

I know what it is like to be afraid of my own authenticity. To go through the motions of your day, wondering when you will be flat on your back with Goliath's foot looming over your chest, ready to squash you. I know what it is like not to be able to trust those around you because if you told them how you really are, they wouldn't stick around. In fact, you know some of them would leave because some of them have already left.

I know what it is like to feel beaten down, criticized, judged, and yet have to stay silent, straighten my back, square my shoulders, and reapply my lipstick. It is in these times when we learn that standing in the face of giants is often enough. We don't need to speak. We don't need to go on the forward assault. We don't need to draw our swords and take an offensive stance. Simply standing is enough. It is *just enough* brave for the day. It is brave enough.

It is said that character is who you are when no one is looking. I would say that authenticity is who you are when you are standing completely alone, facing whatever giant is in your face.

For over a year of my life, I didn't feel brave. In fact, I felt quite the opposite. I felt exceptionally alone, misunderstood, ridiculed, and lost. I clung to my husband and kids, as well as a few friends I could count on one hand. They kept telling me the same thing: "Hold on, Sasha. Remain, Sasha. Stand, Sasha."

Sometimes standing didn't feel like enough. I felt I should do more, fight back somehow, even though I had no fight left in me. It wasn't pretty. It wasn't as if I were a superhero in a cape and pink heels. I wasn't running across a war zone, exterminating the enemy with my superweapon and leaving a trail of conquered evil in the wake of my power. I didn't have a bright and shiny sword to slay dragons. I could barely stand.

There were days when I hid. Behind yoga pants, lattes, green scrubs, and surgical masks. I hunkered down in my job, smiled, and took care of patients as I knew how. I went to soccer games and dance competitions and smiled and nodded at others while crying myself to sleep at night and waking up at 3:00 AM with immense anxiety, only to repeat the cycle the next day and the next one after that. I wasn't thriving; I was hiding. But I was surviving.

But one thing was true through it all: I kept standing. And I stayed silent. I didn't hash out my struggle in the court of public opinion, and I didn't share on every social media platform what I was going through. I couldn't for my own sanity and growth. I needed to grow, and that growth required obedience.

I remained standing. And slowly, Goliath retreated. In fact, I am compelled to write about it so I don't forget how tired, sad, and weak I felt— along with all the other horrible feelings I experienced in that period of my life. I never want to forget it because there is power in remembering what we've overcome.

I want to remember the immense relief I felt when I was strong enough to take just one step forward. I want to remember the moment I felt the sun on my face again as I looked up and realized that what I thought was a giant cloud obscuring the sun was really a massive force. A force bigger and stronger than any Goliath. The force who had been blocking arrows, flames, and hellfire to protect me. I want to remember how when the battle was over, the force moved back, and the sun shone on my face, and all became clear. He looked at me and said, "Well done, Sash. I got you. See what you withstood? Wasn't it worth it? Now you know what you can stand against. Shine girl, shine. Authentically, as Sasha."

It is not lost on me that if I hadn't gone through that experience without leaning on anyone else for support, I wouldn't know what I can stand up against alone. I would not have realized that God is with me always, standing in front of me and taking the brunt of the battle. I wouldn't have known that hope remains—*always* remains. It is our safety net during the storms. And guess what? The more authentically we live, the more hope we have. Why? Because we trust that we were meant for more than someone else's agenda for us. We were meant to live brave enough.

I learned many things in that period of storms. I learned who I am…and who I am supposed to be. I learned that pleasing people leads to a constant feeling of disappointment, emptiness, and failing. I learned that I must be true to myself, the unique person God made me to be, and trust that He will cover me in the storm.

> *"It is no bad thing*
> *To be lost in a fog or at sea.*
> *When land comes into view again,*
> *You will appreciate it with a keenness*
> *That is denied*
> *To those who know nothing but*
> *The safety of the shore."*
>
> —Sister Monica Joan, *Call the Midwife*

The Safety of the Shore

Through the darkest periods of my life, I learned that I am allowed to make mistakes, that, as a woman, I am allowed to try and to fail. Others' perceptions of who I am and the limitations they put on me is not my problem to solve. Just because following my passion or setting boundaries may make someone uncomfortable does not mean I shouldn't move forward and do those exact things. I need to listen to the wisdom of those who have my best interest in mind, to stand with open hands, and receive wisdom from wise counsel.

I learned who I am when the storms hit. When life gets hard, I need both grit and grace. I need to be able to rise up and stand. I also need to forgive myself, and in the process forgive others as well.

I speak up. I am bold and decisive and a real pain in the butt to some people. I call out bias when I see it, and I am constantly asking those around me *Why?*...which I am sure makes some people want to throat punch me. When someone tells me no, I keep asking. If I keep hearing no, I ask a different person until I hear a yes. If I can't find a solution to my problem or find a path to what I need in the current system, I build my own way.

I am persistent. I am relentless at times, and I know that this aspect of who I am drives some people crazy. It makes some people uncomfortable, and while that is never my intent, it is true.

Here's the thing: I am a confident person. Not because I am an uber-successful human and have it all figured out or because I am smarter than the rest of the population. I assure you, I am not. I am confident in who I am because I know I am loved. I have a purpose, and I am determined to make sure that my time on this earth fulfills that purpose. I wrote this book because I know with zero doubt that you also have a purpose.

You have a purpose only you can fulfill, with a special mixture of talents and knowledge and expertise only you possess. When you recognize you have a purpose, that alone empowers you. It allows you to live out that purpose, which requires authenticity and courage. The more empowered you live, the more authentic you are, the more you become a strong force of change that sends waves of hope to all around you.

It is not to say that I don't struggle with the external voices, the pressure, and the plans others try to place on me. It means that in the pit, in the storm, I learned my mission. That mission involves being an example for other women of how to live authentically and bravely. It is scary, mostly because on any given day you will find me driving with a week-old, half-consumed cup of protein shake in my car, and I likely don't remember the last time I washed my hair. It is scary because I fail, a lot, and require a constant source of grit and grace. It is scary because while I don't have the next thing figured out *yet*, I felt compelled to write a book with the message: Live with passion *as only you can do*.

It is scary because I am a human who makes mistakes and has had incredible wins and serious losses all in the same year. It is scary because I hope to God these words show you how to live authentically, which means I must keep showing up and doing that very thing myself.

Go Ahead and Step, Sister

Perhaps you've been living in the shadow of someone else, using their voice instead of your own for some time. Perhaps you've been letting the plans others have for you shape your future, while you take in all the reasons why you must be as they want you to be.

You picked up this book for a reason, and you found yourself on the pages. Something in you is whispering, "You are more." Something in you is urging you to "Say yes because you are enough. Have the talk. Set the boundaries. Reach out. Ask for help. It is time. Wear the power suit. Put on the lipstick. Speak up at the meeting. Share your ideas. Forgive yourself. Grab the power off the shelf. Tell them no. Make that friend. Take that leap. You got this. You are enough just as you are."

The choice to listen to that voice over all the negative ones that regularly shout at us requires change. And it's a painful and strenuous change, the internal kind that forces us to choose the harder road. But that's the entire point of this book: to invite you into the world of grit and grace. To give you permission to be both gritty and graceful. To tell you that you have every right to take the power as a woman because that is what authenticity requires. You are permitted to be strong and kind, fierce and faithful, boss-lady and loyal sister all at the same time. You can be your own CEO and give yourself the grace to fail. You can take charge and extend kindness at the same time because that is what we do as women. We lead, uniquely, fiercely, and in a new normal—with grit and grace.

Finally, sister, I want to tell you that no amount of money, power, or position can ever satisfy you if you are not living your calling and being who you were meant to be. Listen to that one true voice in your life. If you turn off all the others, you will hear it loud and clear.

When you do, you will be brave enough.

CHECKING IN WITH YOURSELF *Exercise 10*

1) One of the components of resilience is choosing to allow a failure or tragedy to embolden you rather than limit you. Think of a failure or tragedy you experienced. Looking back, what did you learn from it? Write down all the things you learned.

_____

_____

_____

2) If the same failure were to happen to you again, how would you respond differently? Think about your internal voice and how it would change.

_____

_____

_____

3) What is your biggest fear, the one that is holding you back? What is the worst-case scenario if you ignore that fear?

_____

_____

_____

4) When have you been brave enough? How did that feel?

_____

_____

_____

5) Think of your internal voice that speaks truth to you. How has that voice helped you be brave enough?

_____

_____

_____

6) Have you witnessed another woman who demonstrated being brave enough? How did she inspire you?

_____

_____

_____

NOTES

Epigraph

1. Parker J. Palmer, *Let Your Life Speak: Listening for the Voice of Vocation* (San Francisco: Jossey-Bass, 2000).

Chapter 1

1. CBS News, "Margaret Thatcher's Most Memorable Quotes," accessed March 1, 2019. https://www.cbsnews.com/news/margaret-thatchers-most-memorable-quotes/.

2. Katty Kay and Claire Shipman, *The Confidence Code* (New York: HarperCollins, 2014).

3. Hannah Riley Bowles, Linda Babcock, and Lei Lai, "Social Incentives for Gender Differences in the Propensity to Initiate Negotiations: Sometimes It Does Hurt to Ask," *Organizational Behavior and Human Decision Processes* 103 (2007): 84–103.

4. Emily Tara Amanatullah and Catherine H. Tinsley, "Punishing Female Negotiators for Asserting Too Much . . . or Not Enough: Exploring Why Advocacy Moderates Backlash Against Assertive Female Negotiators," *Organizational Behavior and Human Decision Processes* 120 (2013): 110–22.

5. Leah D. Sheppard and Karl Aquino, "Much Ado About Nothing? Observers' Problematization of Women's Same-Sex Conflict at Work," *Academy of Management* 27 (2012), accessed December 27, 2018, https://journals.aom.org/doi/abs/10.5465/amp.2012.0005.

6. Marianne Cooper, "Why Women (Sometimes) Don't Help Other Women," *The Atlantic* (2016), accessed Dec. 27, 2018, https://www.theatlantic.com/business/archive/2016/06/queen-bee/488144/.

Chapter 2

1. Mariel Reed, "25 Coco Chanel Quotes to Live By," *Marie Claire,* October 4, 2016, https://www.marieclaire.co.uk/fashion/coco-chanel-s-25-snappiest-quotes-54026.

2. Tara Sophia Mohr, "Why Women Don't Apply for Jobs Unless They're 100% Qualified," *Harvard Business Review* (2014), accessed December 29, 2018, https://hbr.org/2014/08/why-women-dont-apply-for-jobs-unless-theyre-100-qualified.

3. Sheryl Sandberg, *Lean In* (New York: Alfred A. Knopf, 2014).

4. Swethaa S. Ballakrishnen, Priya Fielding-Singh, and Devon Magliozzi, "Intentional Invisibility: Professional Women and the Navigation of Workplace Constraints," *Sociological Perspectives* (2018): 1–19, https://doi.org/10.1177/0731121418782185.

5. Sandrine Devillard, Alix de Zelicourt, Sandra Sancier-Sultan, and Cécile Kossoff, "Women Matter 2016: Reinventing the Workplace to Unlock the Potential of Gender Diversity," accessed December 29, 2018, https://www.mckinsey.com/~/media/mckinsey/featured%20insights/women%20matter/reinventing%20the%20workplace%20for%20greater%20gender%20diversity/women-matter-2016-reinventing-the-workplace-to-unlock-the-potential-of-gender-diversity.ashx.

6. Nick Huntington-Klein and Elaina Rose, "Gender Peer Effects in a Predominantly Male Environment: Evidence from West Point," *American Economic Association Papers and Proceedings* 108 (May 2018): 392–95.

7. Geoff Trickey, "Self-Criticism Could Be the Biggest Barrier to Women's Success at Work," accessed January 1, 2019, http://www.psychological-consultancy.com/blog/self-criticism-biggest-barrier-womens-success-work/.

8. Carol Dweck, *Mindset: The New Psychology of Success* (New York: Penguin House, 2016).

9. Brené Brown, *Dare to Lead* (New York: Random House, 2018).

Chapter 3

1. Goodreads, "Ginger Rogers Quotes," accessed March 1, 2019, https://www.goodreads.com/author/quotes/290077.Ginger_Rogers.

2. https://www.mckinsey.com/~/media/mckinsey/featured insights/women matter/reinventing the workplace for greater gender diversity/women-matter-2016-reinventing-the-workplace-to-unlock-the-potential-of-gender-diversity.ashx.

3. Gallup, "Women in America: Work and Life Well-Lived," accessed January 1, 2019, https://www.in.gov/icw/files/2016%20Women_in_America_Work_and_Life_Well-Lived.pdf.

4. Parker J. Palmer, *Let Your Life Speak: Listening for the Voice of Vocation* (San Francisco: Jossey-Bass, 2000).

Chapter 4

1. Early Bird Books, "10 Alice Walker Quotes That Amaze and Inspire," accessed March 10, 2019, https://earlybirdbooks.com/alice-walker-quotes.

2. Joseph Grenny and David Maxfield, "One Simple Skill to Curb Unconscious Gender Bias," accessed February 24, 2019, https://www.vitalsmarts.com/crucialskills/2015/08/one-simple-skill-to-curb-unconscious-gender-bias/.

3. Betsey Stevenson and Justin Wolfers, "The Paradox of Declining Female Happiness," *American Economic Journal: Economic Policy* 1, no. 2 (2009): 190–225.

4. Kelly McGonigal, *The Willpower Instinct: How Self-Control Works, Why It Matters, and What You Can Do to Get More of It* (New York: Penguin House, 2013).

5. Michael S. Krasner, Ronald M. Epstein, Howard Beckman, Anthony L. Suchman, Benjamin Chapman, Christopher J. Mooney, and Timothy E. Quill, "Association of an Educational Program in Mindful Communication with Burnout, Empathy, and Attitudes Among Primary Care Physicians," *JAMA* 302, no. 12 (2009): 1284–93.

Chapter 5

1. Fearless Soul, "15 Powerful Danielle LaPorte Quotes on Desire, Passion and Success," accessed March 15, 2019, https://iamfearlesssoul.com/15-powerful-danielle-laporte-quotes-desire-passion-success/.

2. Bureau of Labor Statistics, "American Time Use Survey," accessed January 1, 2019, https://www.bls.gov/tus/charts/household.htm.

3. Elizabeth Blackburn and Elissa Epel, *The Telomere Effect: A Revolutionary Approach to Living Younger, Healthier, Longer* (New York: Grand Central Publishing, 2017).

Chapter 6

1. Mindful Mornings, "You've Always Had the Power," accessed March 15, 2019, https://www.mindful-mornings.org/2017/06/28/youve-always-power/.

Chapter 7

1. Bright Drops, "23 Heartwarming Quotes about Best Friends," accessed April 8, 2019, https://brightdrops.com/best-friend-quotes.

2. Julianne Holt-Lunstad, Timothy B. Smith, and J. Bradley Layton, "Social Relationships and Mortality Risk: A Meta-Analytic Review," *PLoS Medicine* 7, no. 7 (2010), https://doi.org/10.1371/journal.pmed.1000316.

3. Candyce H. Kroenke, Laura D. Kubzansky, Eva S. Schernhammer, Michelle D. Holmes, and Ichiro Kawachi, "Social Networks, Social Support, and Survival After Breast Cancer Diagnosis," *Journal of Clinical Oncology* 24, no. 7 (Spring 2006): 1105–11. Nancy Waxler-Morrison, Thomas Greg Hislop, Brownen Mears, and Lisa Kan, "Effects of Social Relationships on Survival for Women with Breast Cancer: A Prospective Study," *Social Science & Medicine* 33, no. 2 (1991): 177–83.

4. Brené Brown, *Daring Greatly* (New York: Penguin Random House, 2012).

5. Emma Seppala, "How the Stress of Disaster Brings People Together," *Scientific American* (2012), accessed March 1, 2019, https://www.scientificamerican.com/article/how-the-stress-of-disaster-brings-people-together/.

6. Nick Huntington-Klein and Elaina Rose, "Gender Peer Effects in a Predominantly Male Environment: Evidence from West Point," AEA Papers and Proceedings 108, (2018): 392–95.

7. Julianne Holt-Lunstad, et al., "Social Relationships and Mortality Risk," https://time.com/4220323/madeleine-albright-place-in-hell-remark-apology/.

8. James S. House, Karl R. Landis, and Debra Umberson, "Social Relationships and Health," *Science* 241, no. 4865 (July 1988): 540–5.

Chapter 8

1. Women on 20s. "Elizabeth Cady Stanton," accessed April 10, 2019, https://www.womenon20s.org/elizabeth_cady_stanton.

2. Pauline Rose Clance and Suzanne Ament Imes, "The Imposter Phenomenon in High Achieving Women: Dynamics and Therapeutic Intervention," *Psychotherapy: Theory, Research & Practice* 15, no. 3 (1978): 241–7.

3. Mirjam Neureiter and Eva Traut-Mattausch, "Inspecting the Dangers of Feeling Like a Fake: An Empirical Investigation of the Impostor Phenomenon in the World of Work," *Frontiers in Psychology* (2016), https://doi.org/10.3389/fpsyg.2016.01445.

4. Mirjam Neureiter and Eva Traut-Mattausch, "Two Sides of the Career Resources Coin: Career Adaptability Resources and the Impostor Phenomenon." *Journal of Vocational Behavior* 98 (2017): 56–69.

5. Albert W. Wu, "Medical Error: The Second Victim. The Doctor Who Makes the Mistake Needs Help Too," *BMJ* 320, no. 7237 (2000): 726–7.

6. Brené Brown, Twitter post, June 2013, 7:00 AM, https://twitter.com/BreneBrown /status/345178759856545792.

Chapter 9

1. Southern Living, "17 Dolly Parton Quotes on Success That Will Inspire You," accessed April 10, 2019, https://www.southernliving.com/culture/dolly-parton -quotes-success.

2. Kerry Patterson, Joseph Grenny, Ron McMillan, Al Switzler, *Crucial Conversations: Tools for Talking When Stakes Are High* (New York: McGraw-Hill, 2002).

3. Rocio Lorenzo, Nicole Voigt, Miki Tsusaka, Matt Krentz, and Katie Abouzahr, "How Diverse Leadership Teams Boost Innovation," Boston Consulting Group (2018), accessed March 20, 2019, https://www.bcg.com/en-us/publications /2018/how-diverse-leadership-teams-boost-innovation.aspx.

4. Betsey Stevenson, and Justin Wolfers. "The Paradox of Declining Female Happiness." *American Economic Journal: Economic Policy* 1, no. 2 (2009): 190–225.

5. Medco, "America's State of Mind," accessed March 20, 2019, http://apps.who.int /medicinedocs/documents/s19032en/s19032en.pdf.

Chapter 10

1. Times Live, "Five Quotes from Oprah Winfrey's Mandela Tribute," accessed April 10, 2019, https://www.timeslive.co.za/news/south-africa/2018-11-30-five -quotes-from-oprah-winfreys-mandela-tribute/.

RESOURCES

Brave Enough Women's Conference

Sasha hosts an annual conference for women called the Brave Enough Women's Conference. The purpose of the event is to gather, unite, and inspire women to live and lead authentically. The conference, which sells out every year, is unique in that attendees are instantly welcomed into a community of women that provides personal accountability and professional support throughout the year.

For more information, visit *www.braveenoughconference.com*

Sasha's Online Courses and Retreats

Sasha believes that women belong in all places where decisions are being made. She also believes women need one another, and that women should not have to sacrifice their own authenticity or femininity to belong. To accomplish this mission, her lifestyle website provides online classes, information on her coaching retreats, and group resources to empower and unite women.

Visit *www.becomebraveenough.com* for more information.

Recommended Reading

- *Grit: The Power of Passion and Perseverance,* Angela Duckworth
- *Mindset: The New Psychology of Success,* Carol Dweck
- *The Happiness Advantage: The Seven Principles of Positive Psychology That Fuel Success and Performance at Work,* Shawn Achor
- *The Confidence Code: The Science of Art and Self-Assurance,* Katty Kay and Claire Shipman
- *Daring Greatly: How the Courage to Be Vulnerable Transforms the Way We Live, Love, Parent and Lead*
- *Present over Perfect: Leaving Behind Frantic for a Simpler, More Soulful Way of Living,* Shauna Niequist

ABOUT THE AUTHOR

© Kye Imaging

SASHA SHILLCUTT, MD, MS, is a wife, mother, award-winning physician, clinical scientist, national educator, writer, and speaker. Her passion is empowering and encouraging women to be *brave enough* in their professional and personal lives. She believes women cannot be *too* brave, *too* kind, *too* strong, *too* smart, *too* funny, *too* beautiful, or *too* authentic. She believes leadership and lipstick are not mutually exclusive.

She speaks often for conferences, workshops, and retreats, including her annual conference for Women's Leadership. Besides her topics related to her medical practice, she frequently speaks on the topics of career burnout and resilience.

Active in social media, she started Style MD in 2015, an online networking group for women physicians that grew to ten thousand women internationally. In 2016, she launched Brave Enough, a website, blog, Twitter account, Facebook page, and annual conference for women looking to advance in their careers without losing themselves in the process.

A board-certified cardiac anesthesiologist, she received a bachelor's degree in biology from William Jewell College, and her MD degree from the University of Nebraska Medical Center in Omaha, Nebraska. After finishing a residency in anesthesiology, during which she served as Chief Resident, she completed an executive fellowship in perioperative echo-cardiography at the University of Utah Medical Center in Salt Lake City. She also holds a master's in clinical and translational research from the University of Nebraska Medical Center in Omaha, Nebraska. She is a professor of anesthesiology at the University of Nebraska Medical Center in Omaha, Nebraska.

She has published over forty peer-reviewed scientific articles in professional journals, including the prestigious *New England Journal of Medicine* (*NEJM*, June 2018) and the *Journal of the American Medical Association* (*JAMA*, May 2018) and contributed chapters to four books.

In 2016, Sasha was awarded the national American Medical Association's Women Physicians Section Inspirational Physician Award by her peers.

Sasha taught herself how to be a gritty, grace-filled leader and live authentically. She wants to help other women be brave enough to do the same.